YOGA:

(A Sympos

Sri Ramakrishna Math
MYLAPORE MADRAS 600 004

Published by
The President
Sri Ramakrishna Math
Mylapore, Chennai-4

IV-2M 3C-12-2001
ISBN 81-7120-965-3

Printed in India at
Sri Ramakrishna Math Printing Press
Mylapore, Chennai-4

PUBLISHERS'S NOTE:

It is with great pleasure that we place before our readers this brochure on 'Yoga: Its various aspects'.

The articles contained herein were originally contributed to the 1981 Annual Number of the Vedanta Kesari. The writers are all savants who have not only theoretical knowledge of what they are writing about, but also practical experience in this sublime field. Sri Ramakrishna used to stress that the one aim of human life is God-realization and that this can be achieved by a variety of means—"As many paths as there are aspirants." This symposium highlights some of the more well-tested paths of Yoga and provides detailed instructions regarding do's and don'ts.

May these pages enable the earnest reader to attain efficiency and harmony in outer life and profound peace within.

Sri Ramakrishna Math, Madras
Kalpataru Day
1-1-1982   Publishers

Contents

Prologue

In Tune With The Infinite

The story is told of a rich dowager who happened to hear the word 'Mesopotamia' at a lecture and fell in love with it. Repeating the word filled her with immense happiness. Her eyes closed in ecstasy as her lips silently framed that word. She had not the ghost of an idea what 'Mesopotamia' meant. Was it a river or a mountain, the latest drug or a most fashionable disease? She did not bother. But the sound of the word enslaved her heart and a thrill passed through her ample frame as she uttered 'Mesopotamia'.

Yoga is a Mesopotamia. It has become a term to conjure with. It means different things to different men, when it means anything at all. Ask a dozen people what they understand by Yoga — the answers will be surprising in their variety and range. All sorts of physical and mental gymnastics are imagined by this term. Pranayama, asanas, all manner of physical exercises and contortions of body organs go by this nomenclature. Some imply by Yoga different types of disciplines to which the senses are to be subjected. To others it means a series of intellectual practices. According to some the Yogi is one who sternly withdraws himself to a cloister or a cave, far from the madding crowd. Yet others equate Yoga with pure concentration and meditation. Some maintain that severe austerity or **Tapas** is the hall-mark of a Yogi. And most people associate thaumaturgical powers with a Yogi. He must be a miracle worker. Defying the laws of science, he must be able to perform wonders. The more inexplicable the miracle, the greater the Yogi he.

In this medley where does the essence lie? What is real Yoga? Who is a true Yogi? In this as in most situations the Bhagavad Gita comes to our rescue. The Gita is the most competent guide on Yoga. In the colophon to each of its chapters we read **Yoga sastre**—'in this scripture on Yoga'. Again each chapter is named a Yoga from the opening Arjunavishada Yoga to the concluding Mokshasannyasa Yoga. The Gitacharya is referred to as Yogeswara Krishna in the last verse. No other single word perhaps occurs so often in the Gita as Yoga. And Krishna's exhortation to his bosom friend is **tasmat Yogibhava Arjuna:** 'Therefore, O Arjuna, become a Yogi'. Remember, this is not a postprandial armchair suggestion. It is a directive given at a most crucial moment in the life of a hero and the fortunes of a nation. Indeed the Lord is speaking to the Arjuna in every one of us, 'Arise, awake and become a Yogi.'

What then is the Gita ideal of Yoga? The Gita too mentions different categories of Yoga. We are told of Samkhya Yoga and Buddhi Yoga, Karma Yoga and Jnana Yoga, Dhyana Yoga and Bhakti Yoga. This is because tastes differ, aptitudes vary - **bhinna ruchir hi lokhah.** As Sri Ramakrishna explains so luminously, out of the same food stuff the mother prepares different dishes to suit the appetites and digestive capacities of her different children. Gita the Mother also presents different Yogas tailored to the needs of different types of personalities. Sheldon classifies men as belonging to three major types—Somatotonic, Viscerotonic, and Cerebrotonic. There are those dominated by the body sense. They are men of action. They derive satisfaction through work. Next are those whose sympathetic and parasympathetic systems are active. They are highly emotional. Feelings and sentiments drive them. The third variety of men are brain centred. They are intellectuals. Thinking is their forte. So we have the three highways of Karma Yoga, Bhakti Yoga and Jnana Yoga leading to the Summit. And Patanjali gives us a fourth way—Raja Yoga, the Royal Road whose stress is on meditation. This may be considered the military road to realisation. It is a highly technical procedure requiring care and perseverance.

It is often the practice of commentators to divide the Gita into three sections, allotting a particular Yoga to each section. This may serve a pedagogic purpose, but a careful, unbiassed reading of the Gita reveals that no such division into watertight compartments is intended or called for. First and last, the Gita is a harmoniser, its view of Truth and the way to it is integral. It takes all the Yogas in its stride and dispenses them with the same large-heartedness. Again Arjuna asks his mentor to tell him which Yoga is better so that he can follow it. **Jyayasi ched Karmanaste mata buddhir Janardana.** If Buddhi-Yoga is better than Karma-Yoga, why don't you prescribe the former for me? Why do you confuse me? Again Arjuna enquires of the Lord about the relative merits of Samkhya and Yoga. And the Lord drops a bombshell by saying that both are the same—**Ekam Samkhyam ca Yogam ca yah pasyati sa pasyati.** He who sees Samkhya and yoga as one, he really sees. In Sri Krishna we find a healthy allergy to all compartmentalisation and hair-splitting. To Sri Krishna, Yoga like Truth is one, even if scholars call it variously.

This central fact is marvellously brought out in Swami Vivekananda's famous aphorism "Each soul is potentially divine. The goal is to manifest this divinity within by controlling nature, external and internal. Do this either by work or workship or psychic control or philosophy—by one or more or all of these—and be free. This is the whole of religion. Doctrines or dogmas or rituals or books or temples or forms are but secondary details". This is perhaps the neatest summary of the nature of the supreme goal and the way to it.

Each soul is potentially divine. We are all children of the Divine and divinity is our birthright. But we have forgotten ourselves and our birthright and so suffer. We have to awake to our dues and assiduously strive to reclaim it. That is Yoga. The word comes from the root 'Yuj' to unite. The Jivatman has to unite with the Paramatman, the finite has to find its fulfilment by merging in the infinite. The part must become the whole. The term Yoga therefore connotes both the goal, the union, and the way, the Sadhana needed to achieve that union. Swamiji points out that it is up to every Sadhaka to choose the particular path that suits him and he is at liberty to use one or more of these paths according to his need and capacity.

The objection however may be raised—is it possible and is it advisable to combine the paths? Sri Sankara, for instance, is very vehement that there cannot be and should not

to be **jnana karma samucchaya.** Karma is not
to be mixed in any way and in any proportion
with knowledge. There is no question of
combining darkness with light. And it is even
suggested by some critics that Swamiji, though
an ardent Advaitin, has departed from
Sankara's position when he recommends
renunciation and service as the ideals to be
implemented. But this is misunderstanding
Sankara and Vivekananda, the Gita and the
Upanishads. These may appear to make
different stresses but if we study them
dispassionately we shall see that all over the
same thing.

What Sankara objects to is trying to mix
Jnana-yoga with Karma and not Karma-Yoga.
There is an ocean of difference between Karma
and Karma Yoga, even as **aja** (goat) is different
from **gaja** (elephant), as the saying goes. By
Karma, Sankara implies ritualistic activities,
Srauta and Smarta. These are performed with
definite desires **Svarga kamo yajeta.** If you
want to book a seat in heaven, do the prescribed
sacrifices. But heaven is only an extension of
the world. It is still part of Samsara, the life of

repetition and transience. Avidya - Kama Karma is the chain reaction. Ignorance leads to desire and desire impels us to action. The action produces reaction and so goes on the endless ring. To get out of this vicious circle Karma has to be abolished. This means giving up Kama and its root cause Ajnana. Karma cannot be stopped in the physical sense. **Nahi kaschit kshanamapi jatu tishtati akarmakrit**—not a single creature can remain for a moment without doing action. But the Karma when done as Yoga does not produce reaction. In **nishkama**-**Karma** the **phala** and the **sanga** are both given up. Such Karma is done meticulously but without attachment and without expectation of results. It is done not for oneself but for **lokasamgraha** and as an offering at the feet of the Lord. It is done **bahujana hitaya bahujana sukhaya**—for the good of the many and the welfare of the many. The fruits of action are dedicated to the Lord, **Sri Krishnarpanamastu.** Such a deed is like fried seed, it will not germinate, it will not produce sequences and consequences. That is Karma Yoga. And Sankara does not object to Karma

Yoga. On the contrary he points out how that is the way the Lord Himself works—**Yatha bhagavato vasudevasya rashtra dharma cheshtitam.** Bhagavan Vasudeva, incarnated as Krishna, was so actively involved in the high politics of war and peace, but He had no axe of His own to grind and so He could say that He did not act at all. Even so the Jnani, without an ego, does actionless action. There is no **Samucchaya** in his case.

If Jnana-yoga can go hand in hand with Karma-yoga there is no difficulty about Bhakti yoga. To the Jnani who has realised his identity with every being in the universe how can the personal God alone be anathema?

Sankara himself is a standing refutation of the fanatical Advaitism that rejects worship and adoration. He was the Shanmatasthapaka who organised six model ways of doing homage to the Divine. And how many soul-stirring hymns has he vouchsafed to us. Finally, Dhyana-yoga gladly accompanies Jnana-yoga, Karma-yoga and Bhakti-yoga! Dhyana or meditation is common to all these yogas.

This is what Swami Vivekananda has in mind when he recommends the practice of the Yogas in isolation or in combination. The Gita itself treats all the Yogas in the same strain. This can be seen if we examine the description given of the man of realisation, variously termed as Sthitaprajna, Yogarudha, Jnani, Gunatita, Siddha and Bhaktatama. The characteristics of all these fulfilled ones are remarkably the same. Equanimity, for instance, is their outstanding trait. **Samatvam yoga uchyate.** From the mountain-top all the trees in the valley are of the same height. The petty differences which divide most of us are not evident to the Yukta. To him the scholar and the ignoramus, the high-caste and the out-caste are the same because he sees the same divine Spirit shining through all of them. As Sri Ramakrishna would say, they are but pillows of different hues and shapes containing the same cotton. And because of this non-differentiation of others from himself the Yogi is perfectly selfless. He is completely unattached to the work and utterly unconcerned about the fruits. He is **nirasi and nirmama.** And precisely because of this he is dexterous in all his actions. **Yogah Karmasu Kausalam,** Yoga can be measured by the skill and finesse with which things are done. Sri Ramakrishna was almost unlettered. He grew up in an obscure village. But what delicacy and profundity do we see in the words he uttered and the things he did! He was literally an artist to his finger tips, because he was artless. He considered himself as but an instrument through whom the Divine Mother got Her work done.

The Yogi is **dhrityutsahasamanvitah.** He is full of intelligence and enthusiasm, but not at all bothered about how things finally turn out - **siddhyasiddhyor nirvikarah.** To him the world is a mart of joy, for it is filled with the nectar of divine bliss. With his centre everywhere and circumference nowhere, no rules or regulations bind him. But like a perfect dancer he never takes a false step. The Gita gives a long string of qualities that adorn him. Non-violence, patience, compassion, steadfastness and other allied virtues shine in him spontaneously.

It is to be remembered here that just as Yoga denotes both the goal and the way, the characteristics of the means are the same as

those of the end. Sankara points out that the
siddhalakshanas are also the **sadhana
lakshanas.** All the qualities that radiate from
the **yogarudha** have to be sedulously cultivated
by the **arurukshu.** Indeed Swamiji recalls with
gratitude the gem of an advice he received from
Pavaharibaba - fuse together the ends and
means. The end is not qualitatively different
from the means. Hence the great need to pay
attention to the purity of the means in achieving
the lofty end.

But among all the requisites for attaining
Yoga, the prime need is **vyakulata,** a burning
anxiety to realise here and now. The Sadhaka
has to be like the robber in Sri Ramakrishna's
parable, who knows there is an immense
treasure in the next room. How can he sleep or
keep quiet? His one all-devouring aim will be to
somehow or other gain entrance into that room
and loot it. The aspirant must have that
one-pointed eagerness and unwavering
determination to attain the Highest which is
after all the very core of our being. If that
mumukshutva is there the other pre-requisites
like Sama, Dama, Vairagya and Viveka will be
added unto you.

Indeed Yoga need **not** be thought of as something very complex. It is true that there are many technicalities and trials in Yogic procedures like Kundalini-yoga. But Sri Ramakrishna, who tested each and every Yoga in his own person and attained the Siddhi promised by each, says that Bhakti itself is sufficient to rouse up the Kundalini. Symbolically Kundalini is conceived of as a serpent coiled up at the basic plexus of Mooladhara. It has to be awakened and made to creep up the various chakras one after another until it reaches the Sahasrara where occurs the Yoga or the union, graphically described as that between Kameswara and Kameswari. Tremendous energy and attention is necessary for this psychosomatic exercise. But Sri Ramakrishna assures us that heat necessary to drive the serpent power upwards can be generated by the passion of pure Prema Bhakti.

The fact is that God is simple and the means of attaining Him are also simple. But we in our grossness have a mania for complexity. If a colourless transparent liquid is prescribed as medicine we will suspiciously reject it. But if a highly coloured, viscous, evil smelling liquid is offered we will eagerly accept it as a very potent remedy. It is our complex mind that sees the Ultimate as complex. This is not to say that there is no intricacy in the highest. But just as the transcendent Reality is also immanent, the complex Truth is also simple. When the mind is purified, the Truth shines in all its unbelievable simplicity. A water drop can as fully reflect the sun as a vast lake.

So the lesson we have to learn is that the practice of Yoga need not be postponed under the impression that, situated as we are in the midst of so many trials and tribulations, the Yogic life is not feasible. It is like waiting for the waves of the ocean to subside before taking a sea-bath. What counts is the earnestness. The Lord assures us **svalpam apyasya dharmasya trayate mahato bhayat**-even a little practice of this integral Yoga is enough to see us across. For those who feel diffident Japayoga is available. Taking the name of the Lord constantly, wherever you are, is as potent a means to realisation as the most stringent Kundalini Vidya. The **Yogyata** for the Yogi is only sincerity and perseverance.

There is however one point about which the Yogi has to be extra-careful. When Yoga is practised, Siddhis come. Wonderful powers like clairvoyance and clairaudition, weightlessness, the ability to become invisible, the power to travel through space, to materialise objects out of the air, are all potencies that accrue as a result of Yoga. There will be naturally a strong temptation to use them.

At first it may be mere curiosity—just a wish to see these powers at work. They may even be used initially in order to help others. But sooner or later the misguided Yogi becomes a slave to these powers. As for a tiger that has tasted human blood, the temptation to exploit those powers becomes irresistible. The power becomes a Frankenstein monster that annihilates its creator. As Sri Ramakrishna was never tired of stressing, that way lies perdition. The Master would say that Mahamaya places these Siddhis in front of the Sadhaka in order to keep him away from the goal. He compares it to the fragments of sweets strewn a little in front of the door of the store in which heaps of sweets are kept. The ants get busy consuming and carrying away the tiny sweet particles outside. Yogis who use the Siddhis that come to them are such deluded ants who exclude themselves from the main store. Miracle-mongering has always been a very profitable trade, but it is spiritual suicide for the practitioners. The scriptures ask the Yogi to look on these powers as vomit or excreta. They are, from the spiritual point of view, reprehensible. Often these powers come unasked for. If a peasant becomes a king, the paraphernalia of royalty come to him whether he demands them or not. But they have to be carefully avoided.

In Sri Ramakrishna's life we read that at one time his complexion was like beaten gold and it is recorded that when he visited his native place, men and women used to stand in the street just to have a glimpse of his radiant personality. Sri Ramakrishna, whose ego was nil, was very much troubled by this public attention. He prayed to the Divine Mother to remove this complextion from his body and the Mother obliged the beloved son. Sri

Ramakrishna did this not only in his own case but also in the case of other Sadhakas in whom he was interested. We are told of one Girija who had the power of generating a powerful beam of light from his back. Girija once used this light to help Sri Ramakrishna in crossing a dark passage at night. But sensing that this power would degrade his friend's spirituality Ramakrishna withdrew this Siddhi of Girija into himself.

Again, one day, Sri Ramakrishna offered all the Siddhis that had come to him to Narendra. Any one else would have greedily snatched at the offer, but the future Swami Vivekananda instead asked his master whether these powers would enable him to realise God. The Master smiled, and said, 'No, but they will give you a high position in the world'. Narendra replied, even as Maitreyi replied to her Yogi husband Yajnavalkya: **yenaham na amrita syam kimaham tena kuryam** "what shall I do with that which will not lead me to immortality?" We are reminded again of young Nachiketas courteously declining Yama's stupendous offer **tavaiva vahastava nritya gite** -you keep to yourself all the cars and dances and songs. I refuse to be diverted from the Supreme Goal by all these degenerating titbits:

Let not, therefore, fringe benefits lure us away from the **summum bonum**. Dive deep into the Divine and be ever in tune with the infinite. ☐

The Fruition of Jnana-Yoga

SWAMI ANANYANANDA

Many are the pathways to God-realization. This notion has been a strong conviction among the majority of the people living in India and following the religion of the Vedas, who are mistakenly called 'the Hindus'. It has been an unshakable faith in the Indian tradition. From the 'dim' days of Vedic antiquity to the 'enlightened' days of our own times, this ideal has informed and nourished the religious and spiritual life of the Indian people. Sages and saints have appeared in this holy land, time and again, almost in every generation, and reiterated this idea in their utterances and demonstrated its veracity in their lives. A Vedic *rishi* declared: 'Truth is One; sages call It by various names.' Descending from the same line of men who were awakened to God-consciousness, Sri Ramakrishna, himself having 'experimented' diverse paths to God and after experiencing the truth of the Vedic declaration, proclaimed in the last century to the modern world: 'As many faiths, so many paths' *(yato mat tato path)*. His illustrious disciple, Swami Vivekananda, the awakener of renascent India, pronounced the same truth, when he formulated the famous statement in his *Raja-yoga:* 'Each soul is potentially divine. The goal is to manifest this divinity within, by controlling nature, external and internal. Do this either by work, or worship, or psychic control, or philosophy-by one, or more, or all of these—and be free. This is the whole of religion.'

In the Indian religious tradition, the concept of the 'chosen ideal' *(ishta devata)* has given rise to diverse disciplines in spiritual life. What is demanded of an aspirant, however, is earnestness and application in his own chosen path, which is suited to his special temperament and aptitude. The *Bhagavad-Gita,* or *The Song Celestial* as Edwin Arnold called it, the scripture *par excellence* of the Hindus, unfolds various methods of spiritual practice before mankind. One can choose any one of them that appeals to one most, and assiduously apply oneself to the realization of the goal, which is One. Like the different radii of a circle, though starting from several points on its circumference, converging at the one centre; or, like the numerous rivers, taking their birth in different parts of the world, eventually emptying themselves in the one ocean, the different faiths prevalent in the world ultimately lead to the same goal, God, by whatever name He is designated.

The principal paths or disciplines are four in number, if we take into consideration the chief strands of the human personality. They are *karma-yoga* (arising out of the 'willing' strand), *bhakti-yoga* (of the 'feeling' strand), *raja-yoga* (of the 'psychic' strand), and *jnana-yoga* (of the 'thinking' strand)—the paths of selfless and dedicated work, of love and devotion, of concentration and meditation, and of knowledge and philosophy. We shall trace the path of knowledge, the goal reached in it, and the 'fruit' obtained by undergoing the practices prescribed for one undertaking *jnana-yoga*.

The word *'yoga'* is derived from the Sanskrit root *'yuj'*, meaning 'to unite' 'to join', and

having the same meaning as the English word
'yoke'. Yoga, as used in the Indian religious
terminology, means the spiritual communion of
the devotee with his chosen deity as in
bhakti-yoga, or the union of the individual self
(jivatman) with the supreme Self (Paramatman)
as in *jnana-yoga.* It should be stated here and
now that the fruition of *jnana-yoga* is this
spiritual unity and identity of the *jivatman* with
the Paramatman. In discussing this subject, we
shall have recourse to the *Bhagavad-Gita,*
which deals with this theme in detail, and to the
words of Swami Vivekananda, the most
outstanding exponent of Indian thought at its
best to the West in recent times, and who has
authored four different books on the
above-mentioned four *yogas.*

True to the religious tradition of India, the
Gita upholds and expatiates on the several
paths leading to union with the divine. As such,
we find the ideas of all the principal *yogas*
sprinkled all over the book, though there are
specific chapters · bearing the names of
karma-yoga, bhakti-yoga, jnana-yoga, etc. For
instance, the second chapter is called

sankhya-yoga, in which we come across several verses breathing the sentiment and spirit of *jnana,* and a few verses touching upon *karma* as well. In the *Gita,* the two words *sankhya* and *jnana* are used synonymously. In the thirteenth chapter, again, entitled *kshetra -kshetrajana - vibhaga - yoga,* we have a long list of moral and ethical qualities, virtues, and graces that characterize one who treads the path of *jnana* (verses 7-11). In several other contexts also, we get glimpses of the flash-lights of *jnana.*

The *Gita* as a whole has been classified variously by different scholars. The most common division of the book is into three groups of six chapters each or hexads. According to this division, the first hexad (chapters 1 to 6) deals with *karma-yoga* and *raja-yoga,* although the fourth chapter, known as *jnana-yoga,* intervenes in between. The second group (chapters 7-12) deals with *bhakti-yoga,* and the third group (chapters 13-18), with *jnana-yoga.* There is likely to be some difference of opinion regarding this division of the holy book. But, by and large, this may be acceptable as good and reasonable enough.

Then there is another traditional classification of the *Gita* by its wellknown commentator, Madhusudana Sarasvati, who also divides the book into three hexads mentioned above. His explanation, however, of the three groups or divisions is interesting and very relevant to our subject. He says the first set of six chapters expounds the nature of *tvam*—the *jivatman;* the second set deals with the nature of *tat*—the Paramatman; and the third set explains the relationship between the two (the *jivatman* and the Paramatman) and establishes their identity and oneness, upholding the *mahavakya*—'Tattvamasi'. An Advaitin himself Madhusudana Sarasvati has interpreted the whole of the *Gita* from the Advaita point of view, naturally emphasizing *jnana* in his treatment. This is not to minimize the importance of the *Gita* for the *bhaktas,* the *karmins,* or the *yogins.* To every earnest spiritual seeker and to every discerning student, there is ample inspiration in the *Gita* for his development and fulfilment.

What is *jnana-yoga*, then? From the interpretation of Madhusudana Sarasvati mentioned earlier, it would appear that the end and aim of the *Gita* is the establishment of the identity and unity of the *jivatman* and the *Paramatman*. Jnana-yoga then is the means by which *jnana* or 'knowledge' is employed to attain this spiritual culmination, which is described as 'the fruition of *jnana-yoga*' in this article. As a matter of fact, this is the culmination, the highest realization, that is repeatedly brought home to us throughout the vast Advaita Vedanta literature, principally the Upanishads. The *Gita* contains the essence of the Upanishadic teachings—the 'nectarean milk' of the Upanishadic 'cow'. There is a popular verse in the *Uttara-Gita*, oft-quoted by the Advaitins, which says: 'In half a verse, I shall tell you what is contained in millions of scriptures. It is that Brahman is real and the world is unreal, apparent; the individual soul *(jiva)* is none other than the universal Soul (Brahman); and there is no fundamental difference between the two. *Jiva* is Brahman.'

Jnana-yoga must ultimately lead one to an intimate and intuitive realization of the significance of the verse quoted above, which is but an echo of the great Vedic statements *mahavakyas*, such as: *Sarvam-khalu-idam Brahma*— 'All this is verily Brahman'; *Tattvamasi*—'That thou art'; *Aham Brahmasmi* —'I am Brahman'; *Ayamatma Brahma*—'This Self is Brahman'; etc. In this kind of an all-comprehensive and universal experience, which is to be felt both emotionally and intellectually, the realization becomes complete and unique. There is a total awareness of one's spiritual Self, which is all-pervading, not exclusive but all-inclusive. In such a state · of transcendental spiritual realization, nothing is excepted or rejected, but *all* is included and accepted. One sees oneself in all this manifestation, all names and forms, organic or inorganic, animate or inanimate, in oneself. The One embraces the many and pulsates in them. Such sentiments are expressed in the Upanishadic literature, portraying the glory of one who has attained the supreme spiritual realization in this path of *jnana* or knowledge. The *Gita* itself proclaims that such a one attains *samadarsitva*, samesightedness; the *'jnanin* sees *all* with an equal eye—a learned and humble Brahmana, a cow, an elephant, or even a dog, or an outcaste' (5-18). Men of God, sages, and saints have testified to this experience.

What are the prerequisite qualities of a seeker on the path of *jnana?* The several Advaita Vedantic treatises speak of what is commonly known as *sadhanachatushtaya*—the fourfold equipment that *must* be present in an aspirant on the path of knowledge. Sankaracharya, in his very popular treatise known as *Vivekachudamani*, mentions them at the beginning of the book itself, after some introductory verses. They are: (1) *Nitya-anitya vastu viveka*—discrimination between the Real and the unreal (apparent); (2) *Iha - amutra - phala - bhoga - viraga* — aversion to the enjoy- ment of fruits (of one's actions) here and here after; (3) *Samadhi-shatka-sampatti*—posses- sion of the six attributes, such as control over the mind, control over the senses, self-withdrawal, forbearance, faith in the scriptures and in the words of the *guru*, and self-settledness or concentration on the Truth; and (4) *Mumukshutva* —an intense yearning for

spiritual freedom (verses 19-27). Having
acquired these moral and ethical virtues by
constant exertion, *abhyasa,* the seeker should
approach a *guru,* a *Brahmanishtha,* one who
has himself realised the Truth, and is
established in Brahman, and seek guidance
from him. The *Gita* lays down the attitude in
which he, the aspirant, should approach the
guru: 'Learn that by humble reverence, by
searching enquiry, and by personal service. The
men of wisdom who have seen the Truth will
instruct you in that knowledge' (4-34).

In his book on *Jnana-yoga,* Swami
Vivekananda gives a lucid exposition of the
whole range of the subject in about sixteen
chapters, presented in a language of easy
comprehension and using a terminology
intelligible to modern men and women. Among
all these chapters, we may particularly focus
our attention on the following: 'The Real
Nature of Man', 'Maya and Illusion', 'God in
Everything', 'Realization', 'Unity in Diversity',
'Immortality', 'The Atman', and 'The Real and
the Apparent Man'. As the Swami expounds
these, he has at the back of his mind some of
the principal Upanishads as a whole, or some

chief thought-currents flowing in some of them.

The seeker on the path of knowledge, both by *viveka* and *vichara*, discriminating and understanding sense-objects in their proper perspective, must eventually arrive at the perception of the one basic spiritual Reality (Brahman) that is all-pervading, ever present, without beginning or end; which is eternal, ever free, ever pure, and all-knowing. It is this one universal Reality that is described as Sat-chit-ananda, existence-knowledge-bliss Absolute. With the perception of that Reality, with the intuitive realization of that changeless One among all these changeful phenomena, that Unity amidst all this variety, which, in truth is none other than one's own Self (Atman) the *jnanin* develops a genuine detachment towards the world, *vairagya*, and turns his mind away from them. He realizes that the Self is no doer of actions, nor is it the enjoyer of the fruits of those actions. Of him, the *Gita* says: While all kinds of work are done by the modes of nature, he whose soul is bewildered by the self-sense thinks, "I am the doer". But he who knows the true character of the distinction (of the soul) from the modes of nature and their works, O Mighty-armed (Arjuna), understanding that it is the modes which are acting on the modes (themselves), does not get attached (3-27-28). In the second chapter of the Gita, verses 13 to 25 describe in detail the attainments and characteristics of one who has realized the nature of the soul. Again, in the same chapter, verses 55 to 72 enumerate the qualities of a *Sthitaprajna*, one firmly established in spiritual wisdom. Towards the end of this chapter, we come across such expressions as *brahmisthiti*, divine state, and *brahmanirvana*, bliss of Brahman, which are attained by a *jnanin*.

In the fourth chapter of the *Gita*, designated *Jnana-yoga* proper, verses 19 to 24 describe the nature of work performed by one who has developed the universality of vision born of wisdom, and who is free from selfish desire. Verses 35 to 38 are in praise of wisdom, and the rest of the chapter emphasizes that *sraddha* (faith) is necessary for acquiring that wisdom (39 to 42).

It is interesting to remark here that the *Gita*, as already mentioned, opens a path to every sincere seeker, whatever his mental make-up or inclination may be, and makes no distinction in the attainments of a *jnanin*, or a *bhakta*, or a *yogin*, or a *karmin;* for the qualities and characteristics attributed by the *Gita* to a *sthitaprajna* (2.55 ff.), a *bhakta* (12.13 ff), a perfect *yogin* (6.6 to 9 and 18 to 32), a *karma-yogin* (3.17 and 27 ff.), and a *gunatita* (14.22 ff.) are strikingly similar. Even the words used in the *Gita* to describe them are almost synonymous.

From this it becomes abundantly clear that the fruit of *jnana* can be had and enjoyed here and now, even in this very life. It is not a state of post-mortem excellence. It is like 'a fruit in one's palm' *karatalamalakavat* as a popular Sanskrit phrase has it. It is this ideal of realization of the universal consciousness while living in this very body, with our eyes wide open, that is held aloft in Advaita Vedanta—the ideal of *jivanmukti*, free while yet living (in this body). The *Gita* itself bursts forth in glowing terms while describing the man of realization who has attained to wisdom in this mortal life: 'Even here (on earth), the created (world) is overcome by those whose mind is established in equality. Brahman is flawless and the same to all. Therefore are these (men of realization) established in Brahman' (5.19).

Such a perfected soul attains equanimity of mind and equality of vision. The *Isa Upanishad* declares: 'He who sees all beings in the very Self, and the Self in all beings, feels no hatred by virtue of that (realization). When to a man of realization all beings become the very Self, then what delusion and what sorrow can there be for that seer of oneness?' (verses 6, 7). In the thirteenth chapter of the *Gita* also, we have similar sentiments expressed regarding one who has become universal in his vision: 'He who sees the supreme Lord abiding equally in all beings, never perishing when they perish, he, verily, sees. For, as he sees the Lord present equally everywhere, he does not injure his true Self by the self, and then attains to the supreme goal' (verses 27,28).

This idea of a universal vision leads us to another important and very pertinent thought-current flowing through the entire Advaita Vedanta literature—that is, the message of fearlessness. It is this message of fearlessness, and consequently of strength and vigour, that caught the imagination of that 'Lion of Vedanta' *(Vedanta Kesari)*, Swami Vivekananda. This is the message he gave to our nation. The Swami was never tired of repeating this message of strength and fearlessness in his lectures in India to his compatriots, whom he wanted to raise from the deep slumber of self-forgetfulness, in order to enable them to stand on their feet once again as a nation.

In his *Complete Works* (in 8 volumes), Swami Vivekananda has reiterated this message of strength and fearlessness in various contexts having a direct bearing on India's social, economic and political problems obtaining in his time. They are equally relevant to us even today. The message of the Upanishads is eternal, and has relevance to any situation anywhere in the world. We reproduce here some selected passages of his, being exhortations in this regard.

'Strength, strength is what the Upanishads speak to me from every page. This is the one great thing to remember; it has been the one great lesson I have been taught in my life; strength it says, strength, O man, be not weak. Are there no human weaknesses?—says man. There are, say the Upanishads, but will more weakness heal them; would you try to wash dirt with dirt? Will sin cure sin, weakness cure weakness? Strength, O man, strength, say the Upanishads; stand up and be strong' (Vol, III. p. 237).

'Strength, Strength is goodness; weakness is sin. If there is one word that you find coming out like a bomb from the Upanishads, bursting like a bomb-shell upon masses of ignorance, it is the word *fearlessness*. And the only religion that ought to be taught is the religion of *fearlessness*...It is fear that brings misery, fear that brings death, fear that breeds evil. And what causes fear? Ignorance of our own nature' *(ibid., p. 160)*, 'This is a great fact: strength is life; weakness is death. Strength is felicity, life eternal, immortal; weakness is constant strain and misery' (Vol. II. p. 3).

'It is weakness, says the Vedanta, which is the cause of all misery in this world, weakness is the cause of suffering. We become miserable, because we are weak. We lie, steal, kill and commit other crimes, because we are weak. We die because we are weak. Where there is nothing to weaken us, there is no death nor sorrow. We are miserable through delusion. Give up the delusion and the whole thing vanishes' *(ibid., p. 198)*. 'All the strength and succour you want is within yourselves. Therefore, make your own future...The infinite future is before you; and you must always remember that each word, thought, and deed lays up a store for you, and that as the bad thoughts and works are ready to spring upon you like tigers, so also there is the inspiring hope that the good thoughts and good deeds are ready with the power of a hundred thousand angels to defend you always and for ever'
(ibid., p. 225).

'The best guide in life is strength. In religion, as in all other matters, discard everything that weakens you; have nothing to do with it' (Vol.I.p.134). 'The Upanishads are the great mine of strength. Therein lies strength enough to invigorate the whole world; the whole world can be vivified, made strong, energized through them. They call with trumpet voice upon the weak, the miserable, and the downtrodden of all races, all creeds, and all sects, to stand on their feet and be free; freedom, physical freedom, mental freedom, and spiritual freedom are the watchword of the Upanishads (Vol.III.p.238).

'This I lay down as the first essential in all I teach: anything that brings spiritual, mental, or physical weakness, touch it not with toes of your feet. Religion is the manifestation of the natural strength that is in man' (Vol. VIII. p. 185). 'So I preach only the Upanishads. If you look, you will find that I have never quoted anything but the Upanishads. And of the Upanishads, it is only that one idea of strength' *(ibid.,p.267)*. 'Strength, therefore, is the one thing needful. Strength is the medicine for the world's disease. Strength is the medicine which the poor must have when tyrannized over by the rich. Strength is the medicine that the ignorant must have when oppressed by the learned; and it is the medicine that sinners must have when tyrannized over by other sinners; and nothing gives such strength as this idea of monism' (Vol.II p.201).

And such inspiring passages from Swamiji's *Complete Works* can be cited page after page.

There is a common saying current among the Advaitins, which declares: *Dvaitadvai bhayam bhavati; advaitameva abhayam*—'Duality or separateness engenders fear; non-duality or *advaita* is verily fearlessness'.

In conclusion, we may bring out certain salient features of this path of *jnana*. A seeker following this path should cultivate the habit of not attaching too much importance to his body or paying undue attention to his bodily needs, gradually developing, simultaneously, a total absence of the sense of ego. He must grow, by constant practice, into an awareness of his essential spiritual Self, which will destroy all his baser instincts. The *Mundaka Upanishad* proclaims:

'All the knots of his heart are rent asunder; all his doubts are dispelled; and all his *karmas* are destroyed, when he realizes that Being which is both high and low' (2.2.9). Another important, but less known, treatise on Advaita Vedanta, entitled *Drig-drisya-viveka*, expresses these ideas in very telling words: 'With the disappearance of the attachment to the body, and with the realization of the supreme Self, to whatever object the mind is directed, one experiences *samadhi*' (verse 30). In glorious terms *Vivekachudamani* portrays the traits of one liberated-in-life *(jivanmukta)* and the 'fruits of endless merit' attained by him (verses 425-441). In these verses, we get glimpses of the nature of a man of realization, who has attained the goal of life, as well as the impressions created by such a life upon the outside world. These verses, again, have said the last word pertaining to a *jivanmukta*.

Swami Vivekananda has this to say with regard to the fruition of *jnana-yoga* : 'The aim and end in this life for the *jnanayogi* is to become this *jivanmukta*, "living-free". He is a *jivanmukta* who can live in this world without being attached. He is like the lotus leaves in water, which are never wetted by the water. He is the highest of human beings, nay, the highest of all beings, for he has realized his identity with the Absolute; he has realized that he is one with God' *(Complete Works,* Vol.III.pp.10-11).

'The Fruition of *Jnana-yoga*' can be described in one word, that is, *jivanmukti*. As already pointed out, what is required of an aspirant is earnestness and application. He must have unshakable faith in the efficacy of the path chosen by him and implicitly follow the instructions given to him by his *guru*. Patience and perseverance in the face of all kinds of odds and obstructions surely chasten the mind of the seeker, and strengthen his moral fibre to undertake this spiritual adventure with a smile on his face. It is practice alone that leads to perfection. Doubting and questioning will not help us; they will lead us nowhere. They will only ruin us, leading to the abysmal valley of spiritual suicide. We must be bold and take the plunge into the deep of Brahman and swim across the ocean of wordly existence and become free—physically, mentally and spiritually. On the shores of *jnana* stands majestically the beacon light of Brahman, beckoning to us with all the warmth that humanity has ever felt or witnessed. Let us not stop till the goal is reached. God help us in our endeavour! ☐

Gita On Karma-Yoga

SWAMI VIJNANANDA

There may be differences of opinion among scholars as to whether the Gita is mainly a work outlining a code of morals—only incidentally touching here and there upon some metaphysical doctrines, or whether it furnishes a complete system of metaphysics dealing with ultimate principles and their relation to phenomenal facts. There may be differences of opinion as to whether the Gita is monistic or theistic in character; and if it has a metaphysical view, whether it is a gospel of knowledge or devotion. But there is no room for two opinions with regard to what specific practical teaching Sri Krishna has given to Arjuna and through him to all mankind. Sri Krishna has left no ambiguity about it. The Gita begins with Arjuna's despondency and disinclination to fight. He thinks that it is a sin to fight against an army consisting of the venerable personages and his kith and kin for the sake of a kingdom. Sri Krishna frees Arjuna from all his despondency by his teaching. Arjuna is made to see the righteousness of the war he is to fight. He is convinced that to fight a righteous war is his Svadharma and not to fight is Adharma. This significant change in Arjuna's attitude towards the war consequent on Sri Krishna's teaching will lose all its importance if we do not regard action coupled with non-attachment to the results as the main teaching of the Gita. So Karma-Yoga, in the language of the Gita, is the specific message of the Gita.

Now let us understand what exactly is meant by Karma-yoga. The term 'Karma' normally means 'action' or 'work'. However, in the Gita, Karma usually means those special duties and obligations which tradition and custom, prevalent at a time, impose upon particular classes of society for securing and preserving the solidarity of society. In other words, Karma refers to Varna dharmas (Chap.IV.15 and XVIII-41).

Similarly, the term 'Yoga', though it has come to have several meanings, means 'applying oneself to' so far as the Karma-yoga is concerned. So, Karma-yoga may be understood to mean applying oneself to or

devoting oneself to the discharge of one's
duties and obligations, without any motive. All
voluntary deeds are done with a desire for some
specific result. In the present case, for instance,
Arjuna is actuated by a desire for regaining his
kingdom. Actions urged by desires for some
particular results would not be Karma-yoga for
such actions would not be devotion to Karma
but to its result. Such actions bind one to the
world. In Karma-yoga the desire for result
should be altogether dismissed from the mind
both during and after the act. Sri Krishna says
to Arjuna 'Your concern is solely with action
and never with its fruits' (Chap.II-47).
Therefore the term Karma-yoga signifies, as
Sri Krishna repeatedly says in the Gita, doing a
deed without the least thought for the result. No
doubt, every action produces a result,
irrespective of whether result is desired or not.
But the Karma-yogi is not concerned with it. His
interest is over when the action is done and
towards the result he is completely detached.

An important advantage in doing actions in
the spirit of Karma-yoga is that one can do
one's actions with complete equanimity. Sri

Krishna explains Yoga as 'balance of mind' (Chap.II-48). When an action is motivated by desire, anxiety as to whether the desired result is going to be obtained or not will surely disturb the peace of mind of the doer. Again, when an action is inspired by self-interest, the doer is likely to lose sight of what is right or what is wrong. Even when he has chosen to do the right thing, undue eagerness for obtaining the result is likely to make him swerve from the path of rectitude; whereas a doer, if he is detached towards the result, is saved from all anxiety. There is nothing to divert him from the righteous path. This teaching that we ought to discharge our obligations, social or otherwise, with a sense of responsibility, at the same time banishing from our minds all thought of obtaining personal benefit therefrom and in a spirit of dedication to the Lord is what is meant by Karma-yoga.

The object of the Gita is to discover a golden mean between the two ideals of action and of contemplation, preserving the merits of both. Karma-yoga is that golden mean in which the merits of both the ideals are happily integrated.

It advocates a life of activity with detachment as the guiding spirit and one's spiritual unfoldment as the goal of one's activities. Thus it discards neither ideal but integrating the spirit of renunciation of the one and the activism of the other, it purifies and elevates man. This fusion of the two ideals in Karma-yoga gives due regard to social welfare on the one hand and on the other leads an individual to the fulfilment of his spiritual aspirations. Thus the Gita ignores neither the society nor the individual. It does not advocate a life of inaction but instead recommends a life of intense action in which self is effaced in all its aspects.

Arjuna's was the path of action. He had come to the battlefield to fight as a true Kshatriya that he was and regain his kingdom. But all on a sudden he resolved to renounce the world and withdraw from war and take to the path of renunciation. He forgot that real detachment was a pre-requisite for anybody who wanted to embrace the ideal of renunciation. Arjuna evidently did not possess this detachment and so he was ill-equipped for this ideal. Yet he thought of giving up the world. That this

Vairagya was not genuine is clear from the fact
that it was not born of enlightenment but was a
result of infatuation for his kith and kin. Real
Vairagya is always a result of deep conviction
that God alone is real and all else is unreal.
Arjuna obviously did not have this conviction.
His disinclination to fight had two reasons. The
first reason is that he loved his kith and kin more
than his Svadharma. He would rather give up
Svadharma and plunge the country into
unrighteousness than fight and kill his own kith
and kin. The second reason was his fear that he
might not after all win the battle with Bhishma,
Drona and many other notable warriors in the
opposite camp. So what looked like Vairagya
on the surface was, at the bottom, only
faint-heartedness as Sri Krishna puts it. Arjuna
had adopted an attitude of inaction not on
ultimate grounds but on empirical grounds.
Arjuna forgot that he had to fight not only for
himself or for his family but also for his
Dharma the interests of which were at stake.
So, Sri Krishna's teaching to Arjuna was that
narrow selfish impulses were to be overcome
and the way to do it was not by resorting to
inaction but by discharging one's duties without

Y-3

any faint-heartedness and without any thought of personal gain. Arjuna was asked by Sri Krishna to shed his fear and attachment both born of ignorance and fight like a true Kshatriya.

It should not be understood that this teaching of Sri Krishna was meant only for Arjuna or people of his time. It holds good even today. Of course, people nowadays may not be so eager to give up social life and retire from the world as Arjuna wanted to do. But the danger comes from the other side. Today people are very much conscious of their rights. In their eagerness to claim and exercise them, they are very much likely to forget or ignore their duties. Hence the need for the teaching of the Gita today is as great as ever. Its value has not diminished through passage of time and that is the mark of its greatness.

Sri Krishna has shown a great sense of propriety in selecting particularly the battle-field for the teaching of the Gita, for, nowhere else the self-interest of an individual is so completely subordinated to the general good as in a battlefield. The soldier may be quite sure of the legitimacy of the grounds on which he is fighting, but he is never sure about how the fighting is going to end. Even supposing that he is sure of a victory over his enemies, he is not sure whether he is going to survive the battle to enjoy the fruits of victory. Yet, this uncertainty does not, in the least, minimise his responsibility as a soldier. He has to do his duty i.e. he has to fight with the best of faith and with the best of ability and at the same time should forget that he is to share the benefits of war. To say the same thing in the language of the Gita, the soldier should realise to the full that he is a doer though he should altogether forget that he would be an enjoyer. This, i.e. to work for no profit to oneself but yet to exert oneself to the utmost, represents the highest form of self-sacrifice and the finest exhibition of this spirit is to be seen on a battlefield.

To be active is the nature of man and the Gita repeatedly says that no one can completely eschew work; for, no one can go against one's own nature. The Gita appeals to men to properly canalise this tendency to work, so natural to mankind, so that it may not be utilised for selfish or material ends and thereby become the means of obscuring from them the higher end for which they are born.

The Gita calls upon all to perform their own duties or Svadharma in the spirit of Karma-yoga. According to it, one should never abandon one's specific duty or Svadharma, whether it is high or low (Chap.XVIII-47,48). It attaches little or no value to the intrinsic worth of a deed that is done by any person, so long as it is not his Svadharma.

The word Svadharma may bear a wide variety of meaning, but here in the Gita it chiefly means performing one's duties which are determined by one's position in society. 'Better is one's own Dharma, though imperfectly carried out, than the Dharma of another carried out perfectly' (Chap. III-35). Performance of one's Svadharma helps one's spiritual growth and also the growth of one's inherent faculties and by doing the Dharma of others, abandoning one's own, one's growth gets stunted.

From what has been said before, it should not be understood that a Karma-yogi has to work with no motive at all. For no activity is possible without some motive or other. So, though the Karma-yogi works without any attachment to result, his activities are not without any motive. According to the Gita, there are two motives which inspire a Karma-yogi to exert himself. They are (1) purification of the self and (2) submission of the self to God's will i.e. self-surrender. Here the question naturally arises: if a Karma-yogi also works with a motive, then in what way are his actions detached? In answering this question we should remember one thing. When Gita asks us to do our duties without any thought for the result, it does not expect us to do away with all motives as such, but it wants us to eliminate all worldly motives and to have the unfoldment of our spiritual nature as the only motive of all our actions. Thus Karma-yoga, though it appears to ignore the personal interest of the individual by insisting on the discharge of social obligations without thought of recompense, does not really do so, since it aims at the individual spiritual progress.

According to the Gita, the goal of human life is liberation. But what is liberation? For a Jnani or a Sadhaka following the path of knowledge, liberation consists in self-realisation, which means becoming one with Brahman or getting absorbed in the Absolute. For a Bhakta, who follows the path of loving devotion to God, liberation consists in God-realisation which means reaching the presence of God and obtaining His vision. Whether liberation means a state of self-realization or God-realisation, its two characteristics are everlasting joy and peace that passeth understanding. Practice of Karma-yoga is imperative both for the Jnani and the Bhakta. For a Jnani practice of Karma-yoga is necessary to obtain self-purification which is a necessary aid to develop an attitude of single-minded devotion and complete self-surrender which alone brings about the descent of God's grace and bestows the beatitude of God's vision. So, whether we look upon the Gita as a gospel of knowledge or devotion, it is equally a gospel of action.

The Gita assigns an exalted position to work. According to it, at no stage of life work becomes superfluous and at no period of life work may be renounced. It expects a man to continue to work even when he has become perfect, there being nothing in the outer activity incompatible with his inner peace and poise. In the eyes of the Gita, mere inaction without proper realisation is as reprehensible as the performance of evil actions and hence it is to be discarded.

A man of realization may not have anything to gain for himself by doing work, but the society at large has everything to gain by his actions. So, with an eye for social welfare a Jivanmukta does work. Janaka and Sri Krishna are two great examples among many of perfect men engaged in ceaseless work for the good of the world at large. So, Karma-yoga has reference both to a Sadhaka and a Siddha (perfect man). When referring to the former, it means that the Sadhaka has to consciously wean himself away from all selfish impulses with a steady determination and when it refers to a Siddha, it means that selfless action has become spontaneous with him.

Lastly what has Gita to say about the doctrine of Karma? The Gita accepts the doctrine of Karma according to which one has to experience the result of one's actions. Some people seem to think that if according to the doctrine of Karma, everything that we do now is the inevitable consequence of what we did in the past, then all moral responsibility should cease for us and all self-effort to improve our being is useless. In considering this point, we have to remember that every deed that we do, not only produces pleasure or pain as its immediate result but also establishes in us a tendency to repeat the same deed in future. This tendency is called Samskara. Whenever favourable circumstances arise, these Samskaras manifest themselves again.

It is in the nature of an action to give its immediate result, pleasure or pain, and nobody can prevent it from doing so. As regards the Samskaras, we have got full power to control them and regulate them as they tend to express themselves in action. While we have no control over our past actions, our present and future actions are controllable. We can make or mar our future by what we do in the present. There is nothing in the doctrine of Karma that either eliminates moral responsibility or makes self-effort useless. It is certainly within our power to transform our nature by cultivating good Samskaras and controlling the bad ones. So, the doctrine of Karma while it teaches resignation towards what may happen to us at present as a result of our past life, fills us with hope for the future. Though the past influences the present to a certain extent, the present is sufficiently free to build a glorious future. □

Yoga According To Mazdayasna (Zoroastrianism)

B.S. SURTI

Definition

The Student's Sanskrit-English Dictionary, compiled by Vaman Shivram Apte, and published under the auspices of the Govt. of India (1963) gives 32 sets of definitions for the word Yoga.

For the purposes of this article, the following definition is the most appropriate:-

"The system of philosophy established by Patanjali which is considered to be the second division of the Samkhyaphilosophy, but is practically reckoned as a separate system. (The chief aim of the Yoga philosophy is to teach the means by which the human soul may be completely united with the Supreme Spirit and thus secure absolution...")

Common classification of Yoga.

The "means" taught and adopted, and referred to in the definition above, are five-fold viz:-

I. that of Faith or Devotion, called **"Spenta Aarmaiti"**, or **"Deena"**, in Avesta, and **"Deen"**, in Persian. This corresponds to **Bhakti Yoga** of Bhagavad Gita.

II. that of Knowledge and Wisdom, called **"Vidva**, or **"Khratu"**, in Avesta, and **"Daanish"** or **"Ilm"**, in Persian. This corresponds to **Jnana Yoga** of Bhagavad Gita.

III. that of Action or Deeds, called **"Varshta"**, or **"Shyothana"**, in Avesta; **"Kunashni"**, in Paazand, and **"Kirdaar"**, or **"Amal"**, in Persian. This corresponds to **Karma Yoga** of Bhagavad Gita.

IV. that of Development of Body to perfection, called, **"Airyaman"**, in Avesta, or **"Tan-durusti"**, in Persian. This implies freedom from disease, and corresponds to **Hatha Yoga** of Bhagavad Gita.

V. that of a combination of the above four, called **"Kshathra Vairya"**, in Avesta, or

"**Khoreh**" in Paazand, or "**Farr-e-Eezadi**", or "**Khudaa Shanaasi**", in Persian. This corresponds to **Raja Yoga** of Bhagavad Gita.

References to Yoga in Mazdayasnian Literature.

Let us, now, take up each of the five Yogas, one by one, and study what is said about it in ancient and modern Mazdayasnian scriptures. Owing to limitation of space, it will be possible to give only one or two quotations under each head.

I. BHAKTI YOGA. (Yoga of Faith and Devotion).

As mentioned in my previous articles, Mazdayasna enjoins un-wavering, un-flinching Faith (Bhakti) in the Greatness and Goodness of Ahura Mazda (i.e.God); in the Belief that Fire is the visible symbol of Ahura Mazda; and, in the immortality of the Soul.

The spirit of Devotion is called "**Aarmaiti**" in Avesta. Like **Aramati** of the Vedas, it is the personification of Piety or

Devotion. The epithet **"Spenta"**, meaning Holy, is often applied to it.

In **Yasna 44:7**, Zarathushtra asks Ahura Mazda: Ke.....**taasht.....Aarmai teem**"? (Who created Aarmaiti?) and then proceeds to answer, the implication of which is who but Thou Ahura Mazda?

In **Yasna 45:4**, Aarmaiti is regarded as Ahura Mazda's daughter who does good deeds, viz. **"At hoi dugda hu-shyothana Aarmaitish"**.

Aarmaiti is regarded as Ahura Mazda's own in **Yasna 31:9**, viz: **Thvoia as Aarmaitish"** (Aarmaiti is Thy own).

Zarathushtra prays to Ahura Mazda to fill his heart with Aarmaiti **(Yasna 44:11)**. His disciples, also, pray likewise to Ahura Mazda **(Yasna 31:1)**.

The Blessings of Aarmaiti (Bhakti)

Aarmaiti makes it easy to understand and obey the commands of Ahura Mazda **(Yasna 48:6)** and helps one to attain **Kshathra Vairya** (Raja Yoga) i.e. God realization. Bhakti Yoga

(Aarmaiti) thus leads to Raja Yoga (Kshathra Vairya) according to Yasna 28:3.

Since Devotion leads to Holiness, the epithet "Spenta", meaning Holy, is applied to "Aarmaiti" (Yasna 51:21).

Those who follow the path of Aarmaiti develop Self-sacrificing spirit. (Yasna 49:5) and Vigour (Yasna 33:12).

Expression of devotion is a sure method of exalting the status of Ahura Mazda in the eyes of the devotee (Yasna 45:10).

Words expressed with intense feeling inspire one to do righteous deeds (Yasna 44:10).

In Rig Veda (5:43:6), Aarmaiti, i.e. Bhakti, is linked with "rta" (i.e. moral order). This means that Bhakti is essential to uphold morality. Likewise, it is mentioned in the Gathas that Aarmaiti increases righteousness (Yasna 46:6). Therefore, a wise person aspires to become righteous by following the path of Aarmaiti (Yasna 34:10). This combination is "a consummation devoutly to be wished" by those who are God fearing **(Yasna 43:10 and Yasna 48:11)**.

Aarmaiti opens the eyes of the devotee to one's short-comings and defects, i.e. it makes its follower introspective in nature. **(Yasna 31:12)**.

Daena and Chisti.

We have seen above that **Spenta Aarmaiti,** the Holy Spirit of Devotion, serves to bring us closer to Ahura Mazda. Devotion to, and Faith or Belief in, the teachings of Mazdayasna is called **Daena** in Avesta, and **Deen** in Persian.

A devotee of Mazdayasna considers it to be the greatest and best of all religions, past, present, or future **(Yasna 12:9)**. It is as superior to all other religions as Vaurukasha (Caspian Sea) is to all waters; as a mighty river is to tiny rivulets; as a huge tree overshadows tiny plants; as the Heaven i.e. Ether, Aakaash, encompasses the Earth **(Vandidaad 5:22-25)**.

A votary of **Daeniaao Mazdayasniaao** (Mazdayasnian Faith) believes:

1.   that   Agriculture   is   of   prime
importance since it involves ploughing the
earth, the guardian angel of which is **Spenta
Aarmaiti,** the Holy Spirit of Devotion. Sowing
corn repeatedly, nourishes Mazdayasna and
strengthens it to such an extent as to make it
walk with the feet of one hundred men, and to
suckle it with the breasts of one thousand
breasts **(Vandidaad 3:30, 31).**

2.   that healthy body and sharp intellect
are essential for the practice of religion **(Yasht
16:16).**

3.   that the white colour is symbolic of the
purity of Mazdayasna **(Yasht 10:126).**

Chisti is an Avestan word which signifies
purity of heart. It is, therefore, mentioned along
with **Daena** (Faith), because one's Faith should
always spring from a pure heart if it is to do
good to the creation and glorify the Creator.
Otherwise, there cannot be a greater havoc than
that caused by unholy Faith arising out of
impure motives. For example, take the intense
Faith which misguides its votaries to offer
human sacrifices in order to propitiate some
imaginary, blood thirsty, goddessess, gods, or

demons. Such misguided votaries are, also, Bhakti Yogis, but in the reverse gear. Their intense Faith, worthy of a better cause, is exercised in the direction of destruction. In this category, also fall the fanatics belonging to different religions who consider it their sacred duty to dispatch followers of other religions to hell with the sword or the bullet.

Zarathushtra, therefore, implores Chisti to grant him the boon of the Clearest Vision **(Yasht 16:2-13).**

Deen in Classical Persian.

Firdausi, the Prophet cum Poet of Mazdayasna (935-1024 A.D.), describes, in the Shah Naamah, how the Holy Prophet Zarathustra instilled the spirit of Spenta Aarmaiti (Sacred Bhakti) i.e.. **Deen** in the mind of Gushtaasp, the Ruler of Iran, towards the Creator and the Fire. One cannot do better than quote Firdausi's stirring and inspiring couplets:

"Yeki paak paidaa shud undar jehaan"
(There appeared a holy one in those days)
"Ba-dast andarash majmar-e oudiyaan"
(Holding in his hand a censer of burning incense)

Y-4

"Khujistah pai o naam-e oo Zardahusht"
(Of propitious feet, and Zarathushtra his name)

"Keh Ahriman-e bad kunish raa bakusht"
(who slew Satan, the perpetrator of evil deeds)

"Ba Shaah-e b iehaan guft paighambaram"
(He told the emperor: 'I am a messenger of God)

"Turaa sui-e Yazdaan hami rahbaram"
(I am here to guide you towards God')

"Yeki majmar aatash beyaavard baaz"
(He produced a censer of Fire)

"Baguft az behisht aavareedam faraaz"
(And said: 'I have brought this from heaven')

"Jehaan aafreen guft bapzeer een"
(The world Creator said: 'Accept this')

"Nigaah kun bedeen aasmaan o zameen"
(Look at this world and the sky)

"Keh bi khaak o aabash bar aavardah am"
(Which I have constructed without mortar or water)

"Nigar taa tavaanad chuneen kard kas"
(Ponder whether any human being could have done so)

"Magar mau keh hastam Jehaandaar o bas"
(Except I alone who am the Keeper of this world)

"Gar aidoon keh daani keh man kardam een"
(If you are convinced that I have done this)

"Maraa khwaand baayad Jehaan aafreen"
(Then, I alone deserve to be called the World Creator)

"Ze gooyindah bepzeer beh deen-e ooi"
(Accept from the Messenger his Righteous Faith)

"Beyaamooz azoo raah o aaeen-e ooi"
(Learn from him his method and faith)

"Nigar taa cheh gooyad; baraan kaar kun"
(See what he says; act according to that)

Khirad barguzeen; een jehaan khwaar kun"
(Accept Wisdom; spurn worldly ways)

"Beyaamooz aaeen-e deen-e behi"
(Learn the principles of the Righteous Faith)

"Keh bi deen na khoobast shaahenshahi"
(Because Rulership without principles is not good)

"Ba Yazdaan keh hargiz na beenad; behisht"

(By God I swear that he will never see heaven)

"asi koo na-daarad rahe Zardahisht"
(One who does not keep to the path of Zarathushtra.)

The last couplet is the expression of the Poet's own feelings and views.

What a wonderful exhortation from a Messenger of Ahura Mazda to the mightiest Ruler of his times! Readers should note that Zarathushtra wants the Emperor Gushtaasp to believe that Ahura Mazda created the world, only if he is convinced that no human being could have done so. Firdausi has, merely translated into Persian Zarathushtra's sermon in **Yasna** 30:2 wherein says: '**Let every man think for himself before believing anything**". Zarathushtra, thus, advocates Reasoned Faith rather than the blind belief of religious fanatics and those who offer human and animal sacrifices.

The fanatical element was so strong in the days of the Mazdayasni poet Haafiz (died 1389

A.D.) that to talk of Love and Devotion to the fanatics was like "casting pearls before swine" (Matthew 7:6). He, therefore advised:-

"Baa muddaee ma-gooyeed israar-e ishq o masti"
(Reveal not to the fanatic the mysteries of Love and Ecstasy)

"Keh bi khabar ba meerad ba ranj-e khud parasti"
(Because he would prefer to die in ignorance thereof, so engrossed is he with the inflation of his own Ego).

II JNANA YOGA (The Yoga of Knowledge and Wisdom)

As mentioned above, Zarathushtra did not advocate blind faith but **Reasoned faith**. This is possible only when the votary of Bhakti or Faith thinks for himself before believing (Yasna 30:2). The faculty of Positive Thinking (**Humata**) springs from Righteous Mind (**Vohu Mano**) and leads to Wisdom. What one gathers and stores as a result of one's own observations is called "**Aasn-e khiradi**, i.e. innate wisdom. That which is acquired by hearing what others say is called "**Gosho sroothe khiradi**", i.e acquired wisdom, according to **Duaa Naam Setaayeshne**, which is a Paazand prayer from Khordeh Avesta.

In the Holy Gathas, the words **"Vidvaa"** (literally meaning Knowledge), and **"Khratu"** (literally meaning Wisdom) are used in the same sense. No subtle differentiation is made between Knowledge and Wisdom because, really speaking,Wisdom inspires one to acquire Knowledge, and acquisition of Knowledge makes one more experienced and wiser. Both are interdependent and complimentary to each other.

In **Yasna 48:3**, Zarathushtra prays that Ahura Mazda may help him to imbibe the best of teachings, **(Vahishta Saasnanaam)** and acquire Godly knowledge **(Spento Vidvaao)** through the Wisdom associated with Pious Mind **(Vangheush Manangho Khratva)**.

In the prayer **Aatash Niyaayesh**, which is in praise of Fire, it is mentioned: **"Vispae-eebiyo sasteem baraeeti aatash Mazdaao Ahurahe"** (Ahura Mazda's Fire carries instructions for all). I have elaborated in great detail, in Vedanta Kesari, of July 1977, what all we can learn by contemplating the beams of fire with a most pious mind.

"Daanish, "Ilm", and "Khirad", (Jnana) in Classical Persian.

The celebrated Mazdayasni poet, Saadi (1184-1292) extols Knowledge in the following words:

> *"Chu shama-az paiye ilm baayad gudaakht'*
> (One ought to melt like candle in pursuit of Knowledge)
> *"Keh bi ilm natvaan Khudaa raa shanaakht"*
> (Because, an ignorant person is incapable of realizing God)

Saadi condemns ignorance and warns humanity against association with ignorant persons in the following words:-

> *"Dilaa gar khiradmandi o hooshyaar"*
> (O Soul! if you are wise and intelligent)
> *"Makun sohbat-e jaahilaan ekh tiaar"*
> (Avoid the company of ignorant people).

Firdausi goes to the extent of warning that:—

M.—4

"Chu daanaa turaa dushman-e jaan buvad"

(If a learned man happens to be your mortal foe)

Beh az doost mardee keh naadaan buvad"

(That is better than having an ignoramus for a friend).

Firdausi's following couplet:—

"Tavaanaa buvad har keh daanaa buvad"

(Able is he who learned is)

"Ze daanish dil-e peer barnaa buvad"

(Knowledge keeps the mind of an old man young)

was inscribed on the portals of the University of Shirav in Iran in bold letters in the reign of the tolerant, progressive, humanitarian, disciplinarian monarch, Razaa Shah the Great, whose mausoleum has now been razed to the ground, and over which public lavatories are being constructed by the socalled Islamic Revolutionary Government at present.

III KARMA YOGA (The Yoga of Deeds and Action)

In the most ancient Avestan prayer, **Ahuna Vairya (Yasna 27:13)** it is said: **"Vangheush**

**dazdaa   manangho   shyothananaam
angheush Mazdaai"** (Righteous Mind leads to
the performance of noble deeds for the Good
of the world and the Glory of God). Righteous
Mind, as we have seen, is the storehouse of
Wisdom and Knowledge.

Zarathushtra declares in **(Yasna 50:10)**
that the acts that he has performed in the Past,
is performing at Present, and will perform in
future, through the inspiration of **Vohu Mano**
(Righteous Mind, Wisdom, and Knowledge)
are all for the Glory of Ahura Mazda.

A Mazdayasni pledges **(Yasna 51:1)** that
he will strive, now-and-always, to express his
inner urges through the performance of noble
deeds.

Mazdayasna is a religion, par excellence,
of action and not inaction. This has been made
absolutely clear by Zarathushtra to his
son-in-law, the wise and learned seer,
Jaamaasp who was the Prime Minister to king
Gushtaasp, the emperor of Iran **(Yasna 46:17)**

Kirdaar or Amal (Karma) in Classical
Persian.

Firdausi, while stressing the importance of deeds, says:—

"Buzurgi saraasar ba guftaar neest"
(Greatness does not consist merely in tall talks)

"Doo sad guftah chun neem kirdaar neest"
(Two hundred speeches are not equal to half a deed).

He, again, makes it clear beyond doubt when he says:—

"Kasi koo ba daanish tavangar buvad"
(One who is rich in knowledge)

"Ze guftaar kirdaar behtar buvad"
(His deeds are better than his words)

Saadi says:—

"Ilm chandaan keh beeshtar khwaani"
(However much knowledge you may acquire)

"Chun amal dar too neest, naadaani"
(If you do not put it into action, you are an ignoramus).

IV HATHA YOGA (The Yoga of Perfection of Body)

In Avestan literature, **"Airyaman"** is regarded as the genius of health. Its name is taken along with "**Ashaa Vahishtaa**" the Amesha Spenta that looks after health, and is more familiar by the later terminology of **Ardibehisht Amshaaspand,** according to **Seeroozah Yasht** (1:3 and 2:3).

According to **Yasna 16:16,** a healthy body is essential for the practice of religion.

The details of physical exercises are not referred to in the scanty literature that is extant, and must be presumed to have been lost with the destruction of the greater part of Iranian literature by Alexander of Macedon in 330 B.C., and by Arab fanatics from 638 A.D. onwards over a couple of centuries. However, from references in Shah Namah to incredible feats of strength by Rustam such as lifting huge, rock-like boulders singlehanded; to Prince Sivaavoush's passing unscathed through a deep column of blazing fire; and the Iranian Mahayogi, Arda Viraf's ordeal of putting hot molten lead on his bare chest without a hair being singed, it is reasonable to believe that the ancient Iranians were conversant with the practice of Hatha Yoga.

V. RAJA YOGA (Sovereign Yoga)

A judicious combination of Faith, Knowledge and Wisdom, and Action is rewarded by the attainment of **"Kshathra Vairya"**, i.e. Divine Power, Divine Consciousness, God-realization, Kingdom of God.

In the most ancient prayer **Ahuna Vairya (Yasna 27:13)** it is promised that: **"Kshathrem cha Ahuraaee aa yeem dregubiyo dadat vaastaarem"** (The Kingdom of God is for him who provides the needy with his requirements). This makes it absolutely clear that God realization consists in Service to humanity irrespective of caste, colour, or creed, and without any ulterior motive.

Saadi expresses the same in "Boostaan" as follows:-

"Tareedat bajuz khidmat-e khalq neest"

(The path to God realization lies in nothing but service to creation).

"Ba tasbeeh o sajjaadah o dalq neest"

(It does not lie in turning rosary beads, or in praying upon a special carpet, or in wearing robes of piety).

Conclusion

Thousands of years after **Ahuna Vairya** was first recited, and this itself was thousands of years before the advent of Zarathushtra, an English poet has expressed the same sentiments as follows:—

> *"If you can sense the one in all creation,*
> *And see the God in every brother's face,*
> *Without respect of creed, race, or nation,*
> *If you feel as at home in a hovel as in a*
> *palace,*
> *If all your Thoughts, Words and Deeds, are*
> *pure and holy,*
> *And everything from the highest motive*
> *alone,*
> *Then, you are right inside the Kingdom of*
> *God, my son".* ☐

Yoga And Alternate States of Consciousness

B. KUPPUSWAMY

The Avasthatraya

One of the greatest contributions of Upanishadic thought is the recognition of *avasthatraya,* the recognition that there are three states of consciousness in the ordinary life of every human being, viz., wakefulness, dream state and deep sleep state. The Mandukya Upanishad, deals exclusively with the problem of the states of consciousness. The Upanishad speaks of the fourth state of consciousness, called the *turiya,* which means the fourth.

Western thought right from the times of Socrates and Plato deals only with the waking state of consciousness. It was Freud who recognised the influence of the un-conscious as a repository of the thoughts, feelings and emotions, which are inaccessible in ordinary waking life, but which persist in the mind and influence the dreams *(Interpretation of Dreams, 1900)* and the abnormal states of behaviour, namely, neuroses and psychoses. He also practised, but gave up, the technique of hypnosis to treat mental disorders.

At about the same time the great American Psychologist William James studied the influence of the unconscious as well as the conscious on religious behaviour in his monumental work *"Varieties of Religious Experience"* published in 1902.

Freud and James made it clear that waking consciousness does not exhaust all the manifestations of mind and behaviour.

Electrical changes in the brain

An important discovery in the field of neurology brought about a big change in the understanding of the nature of consciousness and the processes involved in meditation. Berger of Germany discovered in 1924 that the brain emitted some kind of electrical energy and that this energy was associated with specific states of consciousness. In 1929, after prolonged research, he was able to demonstrate that there are two distinct brain wave patterns, which he named "alpha" and "beta" waves. Beta seemed to be associated with concentration as in doing an arithmetic problem. On the other hand, the alpha wave seemed to accompany states of non-concentration or passivity. The instrument known as EEG (Electro-encephalograph) is used to study the variations in the brain wave patterns. The machine consists of a set of electrodes which are attached to the scalp. There is an amplifier which amplifies these minute waves and there is a device for recording these changes in the brain-wave pattern. Studies in the last two decades have shown that there are four wave patterns: a) the *beta* wave with a frequency greater than fourteen cycles per second, which is usually associated with normal waking experience such as reading a book or doing an arithmetical problem; b) below this is the *alpha* wave with a frequency from eight to thirteen cycles per second, associated with a pleasant, relaxed and passive state of mind when the eyes are closed; c) the *theta* wave with a frequency of four to seven cycles per second, an intriguing pattern, associated with anxiety, frustration, etc., when a pleasant situation comes to an end; d) finally the *delta* wave, with a frequency below four cycles per second, occuring almost exclusively during sleep.

Drug Addiction

Two other events have been responsible for further studies in the fields of consciousness and meditation. From time immemorial alcohol and extracts of opium have been used in order to bring about changes in consciousness and behaviour. However, during the sixties a big change took place with the synthetic drug LSD (d-Lysergic acid diethylamide). Several drugs were manufactured and are being used in the treatment of psychiatric disorders. Tranquilising drugs have been used to reduce tensions, destructive behaviour and hallucinatory experiences in mental patients. Drugs like L.S.D. are called psychedelic drugs as they produce excitement, agitation, pleasurable sensations and hallucinations. But they also produce later deep depression. The effects of such drugs may last three to four hours or longer. There is a heightened sense of

Y-5

perception, an enhanced sensitivity to surroundings and a somewhat dimished control over the thoughts, sensations and memory. This experience is termed a 'trip'. There is an enhanced state of self-observation. There is, as it were, a split of the self into two parts, one of which perceives vivid experiences, while the other is a passive observer rather than an active, focusing and initiating force, reminiscent of the two birds analogy in Rig Veda and in the Upanishads. At the end there is an acute state of depression and this leads to further drugging in order to have the exciting experiences once again.

Popular magazines in United States and elsewhere have carried stories of drug addiction among the youth and its disastrous effects.

It was during the sixties that the Indian Sadhus carried simplified techniques of meditation to the West. Meditation technique was used to combat the drug addiction.

One of the characteristic features of scientific method is that repeated observations have to be made to study the phenomenon carefully and to determine the conditions under which it arises. Though over several decades attempts were made to study objectively the phenomena associated with yoga, little progress could be made because very few yogis could be studied. But during the sixties when large numbers of persons undertook to practise meditation regularly twice a day, scientific studies were instituted to find out the physiological and psychological changes which take place in an individual who is practising meditation. As noted above, the EEG was available apart from many other techniques to record and study the changes taking place.

Altered States of Consciousness

The cumulative result of all these developments has been the development of a new concept, viz., ASC—altered states of consciousness. In 1969, Charles T. Tart edited and published his book with that title. What is an altered state of consciousness?

As noted above, the Upanishadic sages were aware that the normal waking state does not exhaust the field of consciousness. They were aware of the *avasthatraya*, the three states of waking, dreaming, and sleeping. They were also aware of the altered states induced by the consumption of alcohol, opium, etc. Certainly, they were aware of hypnosis. They were also aware of the conditions of fainting, epilepsy, etc. Above all they were aware of the changes induced by *japa*, *tapas*, *dhyana* etc.

It is in the 20th century, and that too in the sixties, that studies brought to the focus of scientific investigations, this concept of altered states of consciousness.

An altered state of consciousness is that in which the individual is aware, as in the dream state, that his thoughts, feelings, etc. or their absence, as in deep sleep state, are quite different from his normal waking state.

In his book, Tart collected and published a number of articles written in learned journals dealing with the varied problems of hypnosis, dream analysis, physiological studies of dream state and the sleep-state, studies on drug addiction, meditation and so on.

During the seventies, further developments have taken place with further studies in the field. Schwartz and Shapiro have brought together and edited two volumes on 'Consciousness and Self-regulation'', the first in 1976 and the second in 1979. The aim of these two volumes is to describe the current researches which bear on the two problems of the nature of consciousness and the role of volition in the regulation of sensory experience thinking, feeling, etc.

Thus, consciousness, cognition and volition have now become important areas of studies in the laboratories.

Self-regulation and Samkalpa

The process of self-regulation is looked upon as a resultant of feed-back procedures. Further, it enables the study of the processes involved in self-consciousness, because self-regulation involves self-consciousness. And the key process here is attention. Another key process is speech. Self-regulation involves resolution and resolution is in terms of speech. This corresponds to the ancient Indian concept of *samkalpa* which is formed from the root *Klrip-kalpate,* to be brought about, to come into existence, to wish, to long for, to be desirous of, to determine. As Monier Williams gives in his Sanskrit-English Dictionary, *samkalpa* is a notion in the mind, the will, volition, desire or definite intention, determination (p.1126).

Thus, the modern studies in self-regulation appear to throw light on the ancient Indian concept of *samkalpa* and its profound importance in elevating behaviour from mere reflex, instinctual or habitual-customary level to the level of self-regulation. As the *Gita* puts it; *uddharet atmana atmanam, na atmanam avasadayet*—Let a man raise himself by himself, let him not lower himself (VI.5). In this verse the *Gita* points out that he alone is the friend of himself and he alone is the enemy of himself. Who is the friend of oneself? The next verse points out: To him who has conquered himself by himself, his own self is the friend of himself *bandhuh atma atmanah tasya yena atma eva atmana jitah* (VI.6). The Russian psychologists and neurologists, Luria and Vygotsky have shown that speech is the regulator of normal as well as abnormal behaviour. First one should tell oneself what one has to do *(samkalpa)* aloud and later covertly. The aim of *samkalpa* is self-regulation. One should not be a victim either of one's self as the *ripuh,* the enemy, or of the other individuals in the family or society.

This necessarily implies self-observation. One should be alert to find the errors one commits in his behaviour and be alert to regulate his behaviour so that such errors are not repeated. To err may be human, but to repeat one's errors is indeed a sign of being not only foolish but being animal-like in one's behaviour.

Attention may be drawn to the famous *Siva-samkalpa*hymn of *Yajurveda*(34. 1-6). In each verse, the Rishi tells himself, may the mind *(manah)* be of auspicious resolve, *siva samkalpamastu,* whether in the waking state or in the sleep state. It is clear that in this hymn of the Yajurveda, there are references both to the concept of alternate states of consciousness and to the concept of self-regulation which leads to integration and harmony.

Autogenic training

In the early 1900's the German

psychiatrist and neurologist Schultz, who was interested in auto-hypnosis as well as Indian Yoga, tried to help his patients to regulate their own behaviour and called it autogenic training. By analysing the reports of the hypnotized patients, he found that two factors were basic, namely, a feeling of heaviness in the extremities and an associated feeling of warmth. He discovered that any one could induce in himself these two conditions voluntarily, that is, withiout being hypnotized. He found that this could be done by the person passively concentrating on certain verbal formulae or phrases implying heaviness and warmth in the various limbs. He also introduced meditation exercises. Clinical results showed that this autogenic training helped in the treatment of respiratory disorders and disorders in the gastro-intestinal tract, besides headaches, insomnia, etc. (Schultz and Luthe 1959 *Autogenic Training,* Grune and Stratton, New York).

Progressive Relaxation

The clinical physiologist Edmund Jacobson of America published his book

Progressive Relaxation in 1929. He showed that mere amusements and recreations do not bring about relaxation. He further showed that relaxation of any muscle implies absence of all contractions. The limb must become limp and motionless, offering no resistance to movement of the limb by another person. General relaxation, he said, means complete absence of all movement, complete absence of holding any part of the body rigid. By using electrical tests, he showed that in complete relaxation there is zero activity of the muscle. He showed that mere bed rest does not bring about such a state of relaxation.

A person lying in bed may indeed be quite restless and sleepless. On the contrary the persons who cultivate complete relaxation report that it is restful and pleasant.

The final aim of the course is to enable a person to be relaxed even while he is engaged in his normal activities.

Meditation as a means to an altered state of consciousness

Several techniques have been utilised in

various cultures to bring about an altered state of consciousness through meditation. As Robert E.Ornstein puts it, "The exercises are designed to produce an altered state in consciousness—a shift away from the active, outward-oriented linear mode and toward the receptive and quiescent mode, and usually a shift from an external focus of attention to an internal one" *(The psychology of consciousness,* 1975, Jonathan Cape, London, p. 107). Meditation, he writes, "constitutes a deliberate attempt to separate oneself for a short period from the flow of daily life...It is an attempt to inhibit the usual mode of consciousness, and to cultivate a second mode that is available to man" *(ibid).*

The ancient Indians have called this "active outward oriented flow of daily life" *samsara*. Etymologically the term *samsara* means *samsarati,* flowing together with, wandering through mundane life. But, by tradition, it is linked up with the hypothesis of *punarjanma*, rebirth and transmigration. The practice of meditation does not necessitate the acceptance or subscription to this hypothesis.

The aim of meditation is to transcend the round of daily living with its pursuits of pleasure and avoidance of pain. That is, its aim is to bring about a totally different state of consciousness.

What is the state of consciousness aimed at by Yoga?

According to the Mandukya Upanishad, the *turiya* state, the fourth state, which transcends the three familiar states of waking, dreaming and deep sleep, is neither *antahprajnam*, nor *bahih prajnam*, nor *ubhayatah prajnam*, that is, its aim is not to make one cognize the internal (subjective) world, nor the external (objective) world, nor to cognize them both. Nor is its aim *prajnanaghanam*, to induce a mass consciousness or *aprajnam*, non-consciousness. Nor is it concerned with the unseen, *adrishtam*, or *avyavaharyam*, unrelated to empirical dealings, *agrahyam*, beyond the grasp (of the perceptual and motor organs), or something *alakshanam*, uninferable, or *achintyam*, unimaginable, or *avyapadesyam* indescribable. It is the realisation of the *ekatma pratyaya saaram*, the essence of the one self-cognition common to all states of consciousness.All phenomena cease in it. It is peaceful, all blissful and non-dual. This is what is known as the *turiya*, the fourth. This is the Atman and it has to be realised. (7)

That is, this is not a mere altered state of consciousness. It is present in each of the three states while transcending them. The aim is to transform oneself completely and to maintain this through all normal pursuits and frustrations in life.

The behaviour of such a person is described in the *Gita* in answer to a question from Arjuna in the second chapter. Such a person is described as the *sthitaprajna*, one of steady and firmly founded wisdom. His mind is not swayed by the sorrows which inevitably arise in the course of life. He is a *sthitadhih*, a man of steady outlook because he is free from passion, fear and rage. (II.54-56).

Thus the aim of Yoga is to completely alter one's personality and outlook so that he is able to face all problems of life with equanimity, while pursuing to achieve the ideals which he cherishes. It is a complete break with normal waking consciousness. It is neither a condition of vain pursuits and frustrations of waking life, nor a condition of mere dreaming, nor even a condition of absence of quality as in deep sleep, but a condition of calmness and tranquillity of mind in daily pursuits. As the *Gita* describes with an analogy, he is one into whom all desires enter as waters into the sea and is ever motionless though constantly being filled (II.70). He enjoys and suffers like all human beings; he has passions, fears and rages like all human beings; but unlike the ordinary human beings, he is able to maintain tranquillity through them all.   □

Yoga In Christian Mysticism

SWAMI NITYABODHANANDA

There has been a persistent effort in recent years to Christianise Yoga. About the year 1960 a group of Christian adepts of Yoga in the North of France baptised it as 'Christian Yoga.' Reviews with the titles Christian Yoga were and are in circulation. Adaptations of Patanjali's Yoga and Hatha yoga were published with the titles 'The Way of Silence', 'The Light of the Soul' and so on. All this shows the power of adaptation and the universal character of Yoga.

The wings of Yoga cover a wide range of spiritual territory extending from the Upanishads, the Gita and Patanjali onwards to later authors of Hatha-yoga treatises like *Hatha yoga pradipika*. Katha, Svetasvatara and Maitri Upanishads mention Yoga—the Katha with the declaration: *"tam yogamiti manyante sthiram indriya dharanam* "Durable mastery of the

senses, that is Yoga", and Maitri saying
"Joining the prana to OM, this is Yoga"

The Yoga mysticism is *par excellence* the
way to actualise and enjoy the sovereign divine
Presence in us, the measure of all perfections
man is capable of. It is also the goal, because the
Yukta, that is, he who has achieved the union,
possesses the Sarvatmabhava—the certainty
that he is in the All and the All in him. There is
nothing more to be sought after. This Presence
is sometimes spoken of in Atmic terms, like
"Ahamatma gudhakesa sarvabhutasaya sthita"
(Gita X. 20), "I am the Self in the heart of all
living beings".Whenever we say 'I, I', it is the
Lord who has taught us to pronounce thus.
Sometimes the Presence is spoken of in theistic
language *"Iswara sarvabhutanam hriddese
Arjuna tishtati"* -"The Lord resides in the
region of the heart of all living beings. Take
refuge in Him with all your forces and faculties.
You will obtain everlasting peace.". For Swami
Vivekananda, the integration with the Divine is
possible either by work, or worship or psychic
control or philosophy, by one or more or all of

these—as he puts it in his royal way in the preface to Raja-yoga.

The soul of Yoga mysticism is to be found in the life and teachings of Jesus Christ, his disciples and the mystics who kept up the Christian tradition. The body, that is the language, is different. The Yoga of primary identity, the Advaitic union of the *Aham brahmasmi* type of the Mahavakyas of the Upanishads is seldom met with. In 'I am that I am', which are God's words to Moses, (Exodus III, 14), the 'I' of God is not the 'I' of every man. Of course, Master Eckhart, the German mystic of the 13th century, makes very bold innovations on this 'I', making it the 'I' of every man, the unborn and undying Self of which Sri Krishna speaks to Arjuna.

Christianity is a personalistic religion unlike the Vedantic religion. The latter is called *'apaurusheya'*, impersonal, in the sense that it is not founded by personalities. Incarnations discovered the eternal truths. The Personalism of Christianity is built on and around Jesus Christ. The philosophical bases to Christianity were given by St. Augustine, the tallest figure of early Christianity and later on by Thomas Aquinas, the most prominent of the Scholastics (Schoolmen). And it should not be forgotten that St.Augustine was from top to bottom a neo-Platonist. Thomas Aquinas appropriated immensely the Aristotelian system to construct his ideas of God, Being etc. in his *Summa Theologica*.

Yoga, union, with the Divine is through the Grace of Christ. "I am The Way, the Truth and the Life. No man cometh unto the Father but by me" (John XIV, 6). Christ is the Second Person of the Trinity, possessing in himself the totality of the spiritual glory and dignity of the Father. The scope and destiny of this union are pictured in Christ's own words:

(i) "I am the Light of the world; he that followeth me shall not walk in darkness and shall have the light of life." (John VIII, 12).

Light here stands for the Logos, the second Person of the Trinity in strictly Christian terms, or for the Son (Incarnation) of God in general terminology.

(ii) "I am the doer, by me if any man enter
      in, he shall be saved, and
      shall go in and out and find
      pasture".

(iii) "He that heareth my word and
      believeth on him that sent me, *hath*
      everlasting life". (John V,24). The
      accent is on hath, the present
      moment and not will have.

Integration with any of the facets of
Christ's spiritual glory and power enumerated
above is productive of divine Grace.

Baptism and the Mass

Baptism seals the union with Christ.
According to the view of the whole early
church, baptism is a sacrament unconditionally
necessary for the Christian. Whoever has
received this sacrament bears indelible to all
eternity the mark of Christ.

The most influential theorist of baptism
was St. Augustine according to whom the
baptised person is engrafted as a member into
the community which forms the body of Christ.
There is infant baptism and adult baptism. The

first effect of baptism is the forgiveness of sins which extends itself to all sins, both to all actual sins and also to original sin

Participation in the Mass is the most effective means of union with Christ as also the important event in the daily life of the Christian.

'Mass' is the common designation for the celebration of Eucharist. The Eucharist sacrifice is a rite for which the scriptural terms are 'Breaking Bread', 'the Lord's Supper' and 'Communion'. In oriental Chirstianity the term that gradually gained general acceptance was 'the Sacred Liturgy'. The term 'Lord's supper' is so called from its particular reference to and connection with Jesus. 'Holy Communion' is so called because of the fellowship with Jesus and the believers who participate in the observance.

What interests us most in the Symbolism of the Mass is the spiritual elevation lived through and the mystical union with Christ obtained. The officiating priest raises the cup of wine containing the special bread to the sky repeating the words of Jesus at the Last Supper as invocation. The belief is that the words of Christ pronounced by the priest, whoever he may be, have the power of transforming the bread and wine into the body and blood of Christ. As the priest personifies Christ it can be seen that it is a sacrifice of God by God himself. *It is an act of spontaneous love.* Those who participate in the Mass and live through this high elevation of the sacrificial-sacramental rite with faith are supremely benefited.

Bhakti-Yoga

Jesus was a Bhakta of the highest order. Extreme closeness to God, whose prominent expression was the life of prayer and absolute submission to His will in all circumstances, blazes forth in Jesus. Mark says that often Jesus prayed alone (Mark I, 35). According to Luke, Jesus sometimes prayed all night (IV, 12). The Gospels make out that both his teachings and actions carried the mark of 'authority'. From where came this 'authority'? From the sense of commission he received from God. When the Pharisees challenged him saying that his testimony was his own and not that of God, Jesus replied: 'My judgments are true, for I am not alone. The Father who sent me is with me''. (John VIII, 16). Again: "Believe me, I am in the

Father and the Father in me", (John XIV,11).
"As the Father hath loved me, so have I loved
you, continue ye in my love".

The disciples continue in the same strain.
John in his first Epistle says: "Beloved, let us
love one another, for love is God; and every one
that loveth is born of God and knoweth God. He
that loveth not knoweth not God; for God is
love. In this was manifested the love of God
towards us, because that God sent his only
begotten Son into the world, that we might live
through him". (I John, IV, 7 to 9).

Of the three fathers of the Catholic church,
St Jerome, St Augustine and St Ambrose, St
Augustine's Bhakti was exceptional. He
reminds us of Manikkavachagar who prayed:
"O Lord, you gave yourself to me and you
acquired me. Who made the best of this
bargain? My body is your temple, my mind....
What can I give you, O Lord, which is not
yours?"

St Augustine prayed. "Lord, I would not
exist, if you were not in me. Rather, I would
never be, if I were not in you, you from whom,
by whom and in whom all things have their

being". *(Confessions* Chap. II): Of Spanish mystics Bhakti's palm goes to St John of the Cross and among the Italians to St Francis of Assissi. The former's originality is Bridal mysticism of the type of Mirabai. In St John's poem describing the Ascent of the human soul to perfection entitled 'The Spiritual Song' the last four steps have striking resemblance with the four stages of human spiritual destiny described by the Vaishnavites. According to the 'Spiritual Song', the sixth step is the joy of betrothal, the first stage of equality of love with God, which compares well with the Salokya stage. The seventh prolongs that state of union. The eighth is the climbing of the aspirant, aided by his passionate love. The ninth is the perfect state. The Holy Spirit infuses in the Bhakta a supreme love of sweetness and bliss. This state quickly leads the soul to the tenth step of the ladder, wherein the soul experiences total union with God. It is evident that this ascent is the same in substance as that of Salokya (entering the domain of God); Samipya (enjoying the proxmity with Him); Sarupya (acquiring divine resemblance) and Sayujya (complete union with Him).

Karma-Yoga

To one anchored in God like Jesus, a contemplative life could have been the proper mode of life. But he chose the 'anchor' and the moving ship of activity. The Son of God is a servant of man. The Son of God has come to serve and not to be served.

We find Jesus engaging himself in three kinds of activity to illustrate the intimate relation between contemplation and action, as also to affirm that the first commandment to love the Lord, your God with all your heart must flow into the practice of loving the neighbour as yourself. What are the three activities?

(i) A great appeal to all. He spoke in the synagogues, he preached in the open air, he taught wherever he could find an audience. His important goal was to make people conscious that the presence of God was a pressing reality.

(ii) His second activity was his personal ministry to the human needs; he

healed the sick of body and mind,
he awakened the faith of those who
had lost hope and the courage to
live.

(iii)   The above two activities have to be
sustained by the force of conviction
so well expressed in Matthew's
Gospel:
"Come to me, those who are heavy
                                    laden;
I will relieve you.
Accept my yoke, which is easy
And which makes your burden light".
(Matthew XI, 28-30).

Raja-Yoga

A   soul   devoted   and   purified   by
Bhakti-yoga and divinely inspired by dedicated
action (Karma-yoga) is ready and ripe to sit
down and meditate. And that is precisely what
Christ enjoins us: "When thou prayest enter
into thy closet, and when thou hast shut thy
door pray to thy Father which is in secret". The
'secret' of the Father is the heart as is often
insisted on by the Philokalia tradition. "In the
morning, force your mind to descend from the

head to the heart and hold it there"—parallel with the Gita instruction 'Mano hridi niruddhya cha'—"Lord Jesus Christ, have mercy upon me."

All of us possess a 'glorious body' which can be made manifest by meditation. Patanjali makes mention of it (Kayasampat) in the third chapter of the Yoga Aphorisms and Vivekananda commenting on Patanjali, says that nothing can injure this body. "Breaking the rod of time man lives in this universe with this body". Echoes of this can be found in St Paul's words: "Your body is the temple of the Holy Spirit who is in you, which you received from God. Glorify God in your body and in your spirit which belongs to God." (I Corinthians VI. 19).

That St John of the Cross, the prince among Spanish mystics, thought in the same way as Patanjali is evident from the parallels that we can establish between Pratyahara, Dharana, Dhyana and Samadhi, and the four *'Nights'* of St John. The 'Nights' are spiritual states of openness to God's Grace. The human 'lights' are extinguished and so they are called 'Nights'. But the divine 'lights' are on. In the language of Patanjali, Pratyahara is stopping the outgoing tendencies of the mind by the conviction that all is inside; Dharana is the choice of the symbol; Dhyana is meditation-contemplation and Samadhi is complete absorption in the Self where all subject-object relation is transcended.

The first 'Night' of St John that prepares the Soul for Grace is the night of the senses. All longing for sensuous things is withdrawn from sense objects and turned towards God. (Resemblance with Pratyahara). The second stage to union is by the 'Night' of understanding. I should stop all conceptualisations and imaginations so that God's Knowledge enters into me. I can do it only by Faith. Faith in God's action that transforms me into His Nature which is immanence and transcendence. (This corresponds to Dharana).

The third step of St John is purification of memory by Hope and the fourth is purification of love by will, the two corresponding to Dhyana and Samadhi. What is real dhyana? Ramanuja replies that Dhyana is Dhruva

Smriti, constant memory of God, which means transformation of our memory into cosmic memory which is God's. What is Samadhi if it is not complete fusion of my will and God's will with the conviction that 'my will is mine to make it Thine'. This is no passive submission but enlargement into the Divine. Purification of love or Night of love, by will may sound strange, but only until we understand the true meaning of Atmasamarpana, the last stage of the worship of the Divine. The self is offered to the Divine, so that the Self becomes divine.

Jnana-Yoga

In the beginning we just quoted a key-sentence of Christian Jnana-yoga which can equally be a key-note of Hindu Yoga mysticism: "I am that I am". This phrase contains more of Jnana elements than the phrase which is often quoted to substantiate the Jnana elements in Christianity: 'My father and I are one"

In Moses' declaration 'I am that I am', God's 'I' is not the 'I' of every man. Among those rare Master-mystics who endeavoured to invest the 'I', the self of every man with autonomous divine content, mention must be made of two stalwarts, Thomas Aquinas and Master Eckhart (13th Cent.), both Schoolmen (Scholastics).

For Thomas Aquinas the intellectual power, though not the essence of God, is a kind of *participated likeness* (reminiscent of the Gita-idea of *Sadharmya)* of Him who is the First intellect. Man's natural powers have to be raised by divine Grace. The intellectual illumination comes from God. By the light of the illumined intellect, the blessed are made deiform, that is like God. "When He shall appear, we shall be like to Him, and we shall see Him as He is". (I John III,2).

Master Eckhart goes farther than Thomas Aquinas. The principal inspiration for Eckhart came from St Augustine. Eckhart follows the 'Neti, Neti' method of Jnana:

Who is the Real God?
Who am I?
What is Time?

Who is the Real God

God to be God must be Being. For Eckhart the classical Christian doctrine of God as creator is insufficient and so he goes beyond it.

"When I came into the world of multiplicity, all things declared 'God exists'. But this does not make me happy, for the same declaration affirms me as created, as creature. Really, I am superior to all creatures, I am neither God nor creature. I am what I was, what I will remain, What I am now and ever. In that break-through I become so rich that God is no more sufficient"

Eckhart replaces God by Godhead.

Who am I?

For Eckhart, Soul is the uncreated Essence which is both immortal and eternal. 'I am my own cause which is Being eternal. I am not what I am because of my becoming, which is temporal. For the same reason I am unborn and according to the manner of my eternal birth I can never die. For the same reason I *was* eternally, I am now and I will be".

What is time?

Eckhart attempts a purification by the investigation on Time. In this he is vitally inspired by St Augustine. "To say that God created the world two thousand years ago, is sheer stupidity. He created it *in the* **Present moment.**"

Earlier, Eckhart has stated that God does not create. He is. He is Act pure. By this Act pure God consolidates the past and future in the present. The three divisions of Time are an open book to Him, an intense Eternity where all movement stops, so also all becoming. It awakens us to quote St Augustine to support Eckhart: "Lord, your today, it is Eternity" *(Confessions XI, 13).* "From the high tower of the eternity always present, God precedes all past time and dominates all future. In this eternity *'nothing happens'* on the contrary, *everything is present.* There in the bosom of this eternity, reigns Permanence, beatitude and immovable Present".

For Eckhart to live the eternal Present which is also the present eternal is true release, *jivanmukti.*

To conclude, in christianity it is not by man's self-effort, however powerful, that he can raise himself to God's Grace. Grace is a generous gift which the Divine communicates to man and unites man to Him. Man can prepare himself to receive the Grace by his intelligence and love, and enter the Life of Faith and Charity (Love). God's Grace comes to those who are chosen. Who are the chosen? Those who deserve to be chosen. □

To conclude, in Christianity it is not by man's self-effort alone... that he can rise... to... grace is a generous gift which the Divine communicates to man and unto man to him. Man can prepare himself... grace

Dhyana Yoga And
Jnana In Advaita

DR. T.M.P. MAHADEVAN

'*Yoga*' comes from the root *yuj* 'to join' or to unite. It means joining or uniting with the ultimate Reality or God-head. Derivatively it also means a path or paths that lead to this goal. It is in this sense that we speak of several *Yogas* such as *karma-yoga, bhakti-yoga, raja-yoga, jnana-yoga* etc. When the term '*Yoga*' alone is uttered without any qualification, it signifies one of the schools of Indian Philosophy, that is, the *Yoga*-system of Patanjali which is allied to the Sankhya school. The Sankhya is a qualitative dualism and a numerical pluralism. It believes in two types of categories of Reality viz., primal nature *(prakriti)* and spirit or self *(purusha)*. These are opposed to each other. The Sankhya maintains that there is a plurality of souls. The goal of life that is envisaged in this system is the separation of the soul from the clutches of *prakriti* and its evolutes. The technique by which this is to be done is taught

by Patanjali in his *Yoga-sutras*. It is the mind,
which is one of the evolutes, which ensnares the
soul and makes it forget its own real nature. If
the modes of the mind are controlled, then the
misidentification of the soul with the evolutes
of *prakriti* will cease. Patanjali includes in his
technique eight steps. The first two consist of
moral training, *yama* (restraints) and *niyama*
(observances of certain rules). The third step is
asana (practice of physical postures), the fourth
is *pranayama* (regulation of breath), the fifth is
pratyahara (withdrawal of the sense-organs
from their respective objects), and the last
three which constitute Yoga proper are *dharana*
(fixed attention), *dhyana* (meditation) and
samadhi (concentration leading to mental
stillness).

The direct means to release *(moksha)* is
Jnana according to Advaita. *Jnana-Yoga* does
not mean here the way of the mere intellect for
which it is unfortunately mistaken by many. It
is true that a keen intellect is necessary for
following this path, but it is an intellect which
has been purified and is rid of all passions.

There are four main qualifications that a person must possess before embarking on the path of knowledge; discrimination between what is eternal and what is non-eternal, non-attachment to enjoyments that are finite and fleeting, virtues like calmness and self-control, and the longing for release. Discrimination means that there should be the skill in discerning the real and not misidentifying it with the appearances. This is *viveka*. Detachment, the second qualification, is the rejection of the pleasures of this world or of the heavenly world, and understanding that they are actually the sources of misery, this is *vairagya*. The third qualification contains six virtues which have to be acquired. Calmness by restraining the mind, *sama;* control by subduing the sense-organs, *dama;* renouncing all actions, *uparati;* fortitude in the face of opposite experiences such as pleasure and pain, *titiksha;* faith in the teaching of Vedanta, *sraddha;* and concentration, *samadhana.* The fourth qualification is longing for release *mumukshutva.* This is in two forms; vague longing and intense longing, in other words urgent longing. It is one who is endowed with these qualifications that has the eligibility for the Vedantic path.

The path consists of three phases; *sravana* hearing the sacred text, *manana* reflecting on it, and *nididhyasana* continued meditation. Of these *manana* can give only mediate knowledge.

There are two post-Sankara schools of Advaita. The *Vivarana* agrees with Suresvara and holds that it is *Sravana* or listening to the sacred text, *mahavakya*, that is the direct instrument of release. The Bhamati school holds that *nididhyasana* or *prasankhyana*, continued meditation, is the means. This school objects that *sravana* yields only mediate knowledge. Vachaspati, the author of the *Bhamati*, who characterises the mind as a sense-organ, says that deep meditation is the *karana* for intuition of the Self. *Avidya* can be removed only by immediate knowledge. Verbal testimony is unable to do this. Mediate knowledge gained from verbal testimony can be transmuted into immediate intuition only by *bhavana* or meditation. Suresvara in his *Naishkarmya-Siddhi* expresses disagreement with this view. Mediacy or immediacy of the knowledge from verbal testimony depends on the character of the object of knowledge. If the content of *Sravana* is immediate, immediate knowledge can arise. If the content is the Self, which is most immediate, we can have therefore immediate experience from listening to the *Mahavakya*. To the objection why we do not have this experience at once even though listening to the sacred text, the answer is because there are obstacles in the way. These may be in the form of wrong knowledge such as taking the non-truth for truth or lack of faith in the teaching of the *Upanishads* etc. When these are removed and are not there the *sravana* of the *Mahavakya* will lead to immediate Self-experience. The example of the ten travellers is relevant here. They cross a river. On reaching the other side they count themselves and find to their dismay that they are only nine. A passer-by who notices their agitation points out to the one who had been counting the group, that he himself is the tenth person. Then they are happy again. Wrong knowledge of being only nine has been removed. Hearing the friend's statement and belief in it, lead to the realisation that they actually had been ten and not suddenly nine as they had thought.

How is the *Mahavakya* to be understood? It says 'That thou art'—'That' being God, 'thou' being the individual and 'art' serving as indicating the identity between the two. But how can the limited soul be identical with the omniscient and omnipresent God? The reply is simple. It is not the identity of the soul with God that is taught. Since there can be no identity between the primary meanings of the two words we have to resort to the secondary meaning. What is taught is not that the soul and God are one. Most of us think of God as with a certain form and having certain divine qualities. We think of ourselves as many and as limited by individuality etc. The *Mahavakya* implies that God beyond form and qualities and the so-called individual, free from limitations, are non-separate, non-different as pure consciousness. So *Brahman* and *Atman* are one and the same. On hearing the sacred teaching of truth in the form of the *Mahavakya* the mind ceases.

The other view, the *Bhamati,* as we have seen, maintains that continued meditation is necessary for transforming mediate knowledge gained from *sravana* to immediate experience. It considers the mind to be a sense-organ. Immediate knowledge is occasioned by the contact of the organ of sense with its object. *Prasankhyana* is the means. By continued meditation the mind comes into contact with the Self and yields immediate knowledge thereof. The *Vivarana* school does not accept this argument. According to it the mind is not a sense-organ. It is an auxiliary for all knowledge. Vachaspati's claim that the mind is a sense-organ is rejected by the *Vivarana* on the ground that since the mind is the common factor in all knowledge it cannot be the distinctive instrument for a particular kind of knowledge alone. The Self, by its very nature is immediate. So why should meditation be necessary for making it immediate? What is *prasankhyana?* It is the repetition of 'hearing' and reflection. How can repetition cause immediate experience? It is not observed that excellence is occasioned in an object by the mere repetition of a *pramana.* If the

Mahavakyas such as 'That thou art' do not have the power to occasion immediate experience how can they acquire that power by mere repetition?

Although the two post-Sankara traditions differ in regard to the immediate instrument of knowledge, we must note that they are agreed on the fact the direct means to release is *jnana,* the path of inquiry.

Let us inquire into the meaning of the *Mahavakyas* in greater detail. Obviously the expressed meanings of the words do not convey the doctrine of identity, as we have seen before. The conditioned individual Self, limited by intellect and ignorance, cannot be the same as the omnipotent Isvara. But when we understand the secondary meaning of the words expressing this identity we realise that both the words in each of the *Mahavakyas* mean the same Reality. Stripped of their extraneous adjuncts the so-called individual and Isvara are experienced to be identical. This is when limited knowledge and individuality on one side and creatorship and Lordship etc., on the other, are recognised to be mere superimpositions on the One Self.

It is most comforting that even in modern times we have sages who confirm the sacred teachings of our ancients. Sri Ramana Maharshi, for instance, is in perfect accord with the position held by tradition. Yet when knowledge dawned on him he had no previous spiritual training. So his teachings constitute an independent confirmation of the truth of our holy lore. According to Ramana, *jnana-yoga* has eight steps just as in Patanjali's Yoga. He explains that the first two steps *yama* (rules of abstentions) and *niyama* (rules for observances) are the same for both disciplines. But as regards *asana* there are no regulations. According to him any posture will do for the path of *jnana*. Any time and at any place it can be practised. In the path of *jnana*, as regards *pranayama*, exhalation stands for giving up name and form; inhalation for taking in, i.e.. grasping the *sat-cit-ananda* aspect of reality which pervades all names and forms. Retention stands for holding on to that Reality, assimilating what has been taken in. The next step being *pratyahara* is interpreted by the sage as "being ever on the mind". As regards *dharana* he advises "retaining the mind in the heart, so that it does not wander, by holding firm to the concept already grasped, which is "I am the *sat-cit-ananda Atman*". *Dhyana* or meditation signifies steady abidance as Self-nature. *Samadhi* according to the Maharshi, is the natural state of Self-awareness. This is *moksha*, liberation.

When comparing the two paths, *jnana-yoga* and the *yoga* of concentration and meditation, he makes the following observation. "The path of knowledge is like taming the unruly bull by showing it a bundle of grass; that of *yoga* like taming it and yoking it". So for reaching our natural state, which is liberation, there is no other means than Self-inquiry. Control of breath and meditation involving mind control *(yoga)* may lead to temporary subsidence of the mind. In his *Upadesa-saram* Ramana gives the teaching in a concise and quintessential form. Action, no matter how subtle or mental, does not lead to liberation. But acts performed without attachment to fruits, acts of duty and devotion, help to cleanse the mind and render it fit to embark on the path of knowledge.

This view is not shared by the *Mimamsa* school. It maintains that the supreme end is achieved through the performance of acts enjoined by the *Veda*. They may agree that release implies freedom from *karma* both in the sense of action and in the sense of the fruit of action consisting of merit or demerit. But *moksha* can only be gained by performing duties ordained in the *Veda*. The seeker of release should, however, keep away from optional rites and prohibited deeds so as not to acquire fresh merit and demerit. He should all the same perform, as long as he lives, the obligatory and occasioned rites, thus he avoids demerit. And when the present body falls at the exhaustion of *karma,* of which it is an effect, one attains *moksha.* So, according to *Mimamsa, karma* is the sole means to *moksha.* It admits, that there are non-injunctive texts in the *Vedas* such as 'That thou art' but these texts have no independent purport. They should be regarded as eulogistic or condemnatory and should be interpreted in association with an injunction.

The reply Advaita gives is this: It is he who has renounced all attachment to works that is eligible to study Vedantic texts and profit therefrom. The fruit of *karma* is prosperity, something - to - be - accomplished and imperma- nent. The aim of Vedanta, as taught in the *Upanishads,* is not what - is to - be - accomplished, but *moksha* which is eternal. When we speak of achieving, we state this only figuratively. In truth release is the eternal nature of the Self. It is ignorance that stands in the way to understanding this. When ignorance is removed there is release. It is no new acquisition, it is the realisation of what is already there. Anything caused by action must be temporary and must have some positive results. These would be origination, attachment, purification and modification. Release is different from these. The Self which is Self-luminous, is not originated, nor attained, nor can it be purified or modified. *Brahman* does not fall under any one of these categories. The eternal is ever there, ever attained, and always pure by its very nature, never subject to change.

There is another view which is called *Jnana-niyoga-vada.* It holds that the injunctions found in the *Upanishads* in which meditation is advocated, are of supreme importance. We are to combine statements on *Atman* and *Brahman* with injunctions on *upasana*. The Self is taught, according to them, but this teaching is subsidiary to the injunction of meditation. Therefore the purport of the *Upanishads* that constitute *jnana-kanda* is *niyoga*. To the followers of this school Advaita replies that it is nescience that is the cause of all evil including the soul's apparent conjunction with residual impressions generated by previous action. If this superimposition on the true Self is not removed by the direct intuition, no amount of meditation can remove it. Meditation is an act and itself comes under the category of delusion, how can this occasion direct Self-realisation?

Although *karma* and *dhyana* cannot be the direct means to release, they are extremely useful in conditioning the aspirant for the final step. *Karma* in the form of religious duty and social service, when it is done without any anticipation of fruit, purifies the mind. And, meditation enables it to concentrate and become one-pointed so that it can turn its attention away from the material things and makes it turn towards the inner Self.

Dhyana-yoga, no doubt is very helpful to the path of knowledge. The author of the *Panchadasi,* however, compares *Dhyana-Yoga* to *Samvadi-bhrama* which is a delusion yielding nevertheless a fruitful result. The example given is that both the light of the lamp and the light of a gem may be mistaken for a gem. Both are cases of equal delusion. But the person who mistakes the light of the lamp for a gem and approaches it finds nothing valuable, whereas the one who mistakes the light of a gem for the gem itself gets the gem. So the last case is a delusion which comes true. The path of meditation should not be underestimated, the reason being that most of us are not ready to follow the path of knowledge. Only, *dhyana-yoga* must be considered in proper proportion regarding the final method towards release.

Although in the *Panchadasi* a chapter is devoted to *dhyana-yoga,* where it is compared to *samvadi-bhrama,* this text does not differ from the main position of Advaita that *jnana* is the direct means to release. ☐

Laya Yoga

SWAMI SHRADHANANDA

The word Laya means dissolution — disintegration of the gross into the fine, — disappearance of the effect into the cause. Laya is as important as Srishti or Creation and Sthiti or sustenance in the cosmic process. According to Hindu tradition, God has to be worshipped not merely as the creator and supporter of the universe, but also as its destroyer. The Chandogya Upanishad, for example, prescribes:

> All this is Brahman. Meditate
> calmly on Him as the One from
> whom everything is born, by whom
> everything is maintained and annihilated.[1]

In the eleventh chapter of the Gita we find a tangible picture of God's cosmic destructive action. Arjuna sees that within God's cosmic body not merely all segments of the universe and all types of beings including gods and angels are functioning, but simultaneously the terrible power of death and dissolution is also in full sway.

Verily, as the many torrents of rivers flow towards the ocean, so do these heroes in the world of men enter Thy mouths fiercely flaming on all sides.

As moths speedily rush into a blazing fire to perish, just so do these creatures also rush into Thy mouths fast, only to be destroyed.

Trembling with fear Arjuna asks, "Tell me who Thou art, fierce in form?" Sri Bhagavan says, "I am the mighty world destroying Time here made manifest for the purpose of demolishing the world."[2]

The above are examples of God's forms of destruction. We can also remember the form of Maha Kali. Along with the expressions of boon and fearlessness in Her two hands, we see in the other two hands symbols of death like the sword and the severed human skull.

The Bhagavad Gita speaks of the cosmic dissolution thus: 'The very same multitude of beings (that existed in the preceding day of Brahma) being born again and again, merge, in spite of themselves, O Son of Pritha, (into the unmanifested), at the approach of the night (of Brahma) and remanifest at the approach of day."[3]

Brahma in Hindu thought is the cosmic individual having the whole universe as his body. He rules and watches the emergence and dissolution of the universe in cyclic order. A human being (Jiva) too goes through the same experience of appearance and disappearance of phenomena everyday in his life in the cycle of waking and sleep.

Laya Yoga in General

These ideas of dissolution, if included in our contemplation, form the first steps of Laya-Yoga. Normally, we are very much attached to the world, which is very real to us. We love our life, centred in our body and mind, and the stage of this world where the drama of our life is enacted. We shudder to think of the termination of this drama. This is, of course, irrational, because the curtain is bound to drop one day. In spite of longing for life, death cannot be prevented.

The Yogi, who is trying to solve the mystery of life and realize the supreme truth, cannot afford to be irrational. He has to examine the contradictions of our thinking and behaviour. So he faces creation but does not ignore dissolution. He has learnt from the scriptures, as also from everyday experience, that Laya is a potent factor of the world process. Truth is above the duality of life and death. So he calmly reflects on the ever-changing, ever-dissolving nature of the world and pins his hope on the unchanging reality at the back of the flux. Practice of this contemplation brings a serenity of mind based on Vairagyam, detachment.

The first verse of the Isa Upanishad says:
All the changing things and
events of this world have to be
covered with Isa (God—the Supreme
Reality). Live your life in a spirit of
non-attachment. Don't crave for
possessions which are not yours.[4]

Laya in Bhakti Yoga

A Bhakta (devotee) wants to love God. For him God is the totality of all love. In that love for the Supreme, all human aspirations are culminated. Worship, Prayer, Japa (repetition of the holy name) and numerous other positive practices are enjoined in the scriptures for the cultivation of Bhakti. But in order that these practices become really effective, a great obstacle has to be surmounted first, namely, our deep attachment to the world of senses. A Sattvika state of mind, which is essential for the development of Divine love, cannot be attained if the mind is constantly tossed by worldly attractions. Here, Laya Yoga can be of immense help. Continuously contemplating on the transitoriness of things, the Bhakta establishes a spiritually healthy attitude towards the world—which no longer appears to be our permanent abode. God alone is real and all things of the world are passing shadows. With this conviction, the Rajasik and Tamasik elements of the mind are considerably reduced and the ground is ready for a genuine growth of Bhakti. A Bhakta practising Laya-Yoga includes in his contemplation God's Divine glory as

Death. "I am the all-demolishing Death—says
Bhagavan Sri Krishna."

(Gita 10.34)

In numerous hymns of the Puranas, we
find God praised not merely as the creator and
supporter of the universe, but also as its
destroyer. In the eleventh chapter of Srimad
Bhagavatam, the gods are described to be
singing the glory of Lord Sri Krishna thus:

> Thou art the great Time—the
> agent for the appearance, conti-
> nuance and dissolution of the worlds.
> The sages describe Thee as greater
> than the unmanifest, the manifest
> and the subtle. Thou art the
> Supreme Person now engaged in the
> disintegration of everything, acting
> as the all-devouring three-limbed
> Time with immeasurable speed.[5]

A devotee has also to practise the gradual
Laya of his ego. In his perspective of life, God is
the ultimate doer. The self-assertion of the ego
may be important in practical Mayic life, but it is
a monstrous stumbling block in the path of

devotion. Everytime the ego shouts 'I' or 'mine' the devotee has to hammer it till its voice is stilled into the Power which is God. The more he is able to dissolve his ego, the more he becomes conscious of God's presence in his body and mind.

Likewise, the Bhakta has to practise Laya of his strong desires and sense experiences. The Sandilya Vidya (meditation according to the sage Sandilya) in the Chandogya Upanishad prescribes that Brahman has to be meditated as Sarvakarma—the promoter of all actions, Sarvakama—the source and the ultimate goal of all desires, Sarvagandha—the possessor of all agreeable odours, Sarvarasa—the holder of all pleasant tastes.[6] God is the Sarva—totality. So the meditator has to dissolve all separate sensations and feelings into the whole which is God. This will minimize the distractions of his mind and keep it steady on the object of his foremost love—God.

Laya in Karma Yoga

Karma or action is normally distractive and leading to more and more worldly bondage because of our attachment to the fruits of our

actions. A spritual seeker need not shirk Karma
but has to learn to do it in the Yogic way. The
Bhagavad Gita indicates the principal technique
of Karma Yoga. 'You have right only for the
work undertaken, but never for its fruits.'[7] So
the Karma Yogi has to continuously relinquish
his attachment for the results of his actions.
Work for the Karma Yogi is Yajna or holy
sacrifice. The oblations for this sacrifice are his
attachments and sense of agency.

Swami Vivekananda prescribed: "Throw
self overboard and work." Work motivated by
selfish attachment shuts off the light of truth.
When this attachment is dissolved by tireless
effort, Karma paves the way to spiritual
tranquillity. All actions are really coming from
God, says the Gita (18.46), and the spiritual
seeker therefore should offer all his Karma to
God. Karma Yoga finally takes one to the stage
when Karma itself, with all its distracting and
binding factors, melts away.

> Devoid of attachment, free
> from the thought of gain or loss,
> with mind centred in knowledge
> and performing work for Yajna

alone, his whole Karma dissolves
away[8]

Elsewhere in the Gita we read that "Just as
a blazing fire reduces wood into ashes, so does
the fire of knowledge burn all Karma into
ashes." (Gita 4.27)

Laya in Advaita Vedanta

Advaita or non-dualistic Vedanta seeks to
rise above Saguna Brahman (God with
attributes) and reach the Absolute—Nirguna
(God free from all attributes) which is one with
the true Self of man. Upanishads declare the
identity of Self with the Nirguna Brahman by the
Maha-Vakyas, the great sentences such as
Aham   Brahmasmi—I   am   Brahman,
Tattvamasi—Thou art That, and so on.

Laya in Jnana-Yoga with the techniques of
successive elimination of all forms of duality is
the basic spiritual practice for the above end.
The vast external universe with its endless
segments perceived through our senses, the
internal world of thoughts, emotions and
desires, our own individuality centred in our
body and mind, finally Saguna Brahman, God

with attributes, whom we consider the creator and ruler of everything and with whom we commune through prayers and meditations — this trio of Jagat - Jiva - Iswara — world (external and internal) — the individual person — God is declared by Advaita Vedanta as Dvaitam — duality. "There is fear indeed from the second" says the Brihadaranyaka Upanishad (1.4.2).

The Jnana-Yogi through Vichara, reflective analysis and contemplation, seeks to gradually eliminate all shades of duality from his experience and stand on the non-dual Truth which is his true Self. This is not an easy task, because the accumulated Samskaras (impressions) of the mind all the time force us to accept the reality of the manifold world of experience.

The method of the Upanishads for achieving the ultimate goal, Unity, is gradual reconditioning of the mind through the practice of specific contemplations. The mind is a tool both of ignorance and knowledge. Left to itself the mind is engaged only in the manifold; but the same mind, when trained and expanded, can comprehend more and more glimpses of Unity. In the sixth chapter of the Chandogya Upanishad, a father who is an illumined person begins teaching his son, Svetaketu, by taking some well-known examples. In the jeweller's shop there are ornaments of different shapes and names—each different from the other. If, however, you concentrate on the material of these articles, namely gold, and ignore the outward forms, you at once find the underlying Unity among the numerous articles of jewellery. The same is the case with the material clay and articles made of clay, the material iron and all implements fashioned out of it. In the same way, the seeker in his meditation should direct his mind to the spiritual reality *Sat*—of which everything is made. He should continuously try to dissolve the names and forms into the ground of all existence, Brahman as 'Sat'.

The experience of deep sleep affords another clue to Unity. In deep sleep, there is no cognition of the external world or of the mind and the ego. "The individuality has merged into

Sat."[9] The deep sleep experience, if seriously reflected on, is bound to convince us that names and forms can disappear under certain situations. Disappearance of duality in deep sleep is a bio-psychological process which comes naturally, not merely to human beings, but also to animals. The Upanishads never imply that the deep sleep experience is spiritual knowledge of Advaitam but the experience if earnestly viewed, certainly takes away much of our waking bias, namely, all that is meaningful in life is our waking world.

Svetaketu in the above mentioned sixth chapter of the Chandogya Upanishad has further shown three more examples from everyday life in the practice of Laya Yoga. (1) Rivers from diverse directions flow into the ocean and become one with the ocean. (2) Bees make honey by collecting juices from various flowers and reduce them into one essence where the particular identities of the juices are lost. (3) Salt put into a jar of water dissolves and becomes one with the water, losing its specific form. The father then concluded:

That Being (Sat) which is the
subtle essence—in it all that exists
has its Self. That is the Truth. That
is Atman. That thou art, O Svetaketu.[10]

In the third chapter of the Taittiriya
Upanishad (Bhriguvalli) Bhrigu asks his father
Varuna to teach him the Knowledge of
Brahman. Before describing the nature of
Brahman Varuna prescribes to his son the
purification of the body, Prana or the
life-principle, senses like the eyes and the ears,
the mind and speech.[11] Then the father
instructs:

Crave to know that from which
all these beings take birth, by which
they live after being born and towards which they move and into
which they merge. That is Brahman.[12]

Since it is difficult to grasp the Supreme
reality all at once, Bhrigu was advised to practise
different grades of Unity. The first exercise was
to meditate on Annam—the totality of all

material bodies as Brahman. During this meditation, the mind has to merge all individual bodies into that total gross entity which elsewhere in the Upanishads has been described as Virat. After grasping this gross aspect of Unity, Bhrigu was ready for the next step—to know Brahman as Cosmic Life Principle. Since any form of life can be considered to be a part of the all—pervading Cosmic Life, Bhrigu had by the technique of Laya Yoga absorbed all individual manifestations of Prana into the whole which is Prana Brahman. The following three steps were the meditation of mind, Vijnanam—intelligence of Ananda—joy as Brahman. All mental modifications manifesting in myriads of individual minds had to be drowned into the Cosmic Mind, now described as Brahman. All particular 'Vijnanam'—pieces of knowledge—were absorbed into Vijnana-Brahman, Knowledge Brahman. Finally every conceivable pleasure or delight was merged into Brahman as Ananda.

In the above mentioned cases, the Unity sought was of course partial, but even this partial comprehension of Unity is a great step to the Supreme Knowledge of Brahman.

If by Viveka, discrimination, the extreme transience and instability of things have been determined, and by Vairagyam, dispassion, morbid and irrational attachment to the world has been attenuated and if Sama and Dama, control of mind and senses, Shraddha, faith in the scriptures and in the words of the Guru, and Mumukshutvam, keen desire for freedom, have become constant companions of the spiritual seeker, the ground is at last ready to undertake the terminal feat of Laya which Vedanta calls Apavada—complete dissolution of duality into the non-dual Self. The Sadhaka has to continue his practice relentlessly with courage and determination. Success is assured, declare the Vedantic scriptures and illumined teachers. The non-dual experience is usually called Nirvikalpa Samadhi—complete quiescence.

The Mundaka Upanishad Says:
   The fifteen constituents (of the
   body) go back to their causes, and
   all the senses to their respective

deities; the actions and the limited intelligent self (Jivatma) become one with the highest imperishable Brahman, which is the Self of all.[13]

Narendra, the future Vivekananda, expressed to Sri Ramakrishna in the Cossipore garden house his desire to stay in the state of Nirvikalpa Samadhi as long as he liked. Sri Ramakrishna smiled and said that there was a higher goal than that—the application of the non-dual knowledge of Samadhi to the world of multiplicity. After coming down from Samadhi, the Sadhaka must be able to see that the multiplicity was nothing else but Brahman, and if he is of a compassionate heart, he should devote himself to the service of God in the many. This view of Sri Ramakrishna is authenticated by passages of Vedantic scriptures. The Chandogya Upanishad describes the experience of an illumined sage:

> From the dark (the incomprehensible Unity realized in the heart) I come down to the variegated, from the variegated again I go to the

dark. Shaking off evil as a horse
(the dirt from) his hairs, shaking off
the body as the moon frees itself
from the mouth of Rahu, I having
fulfilled all ends am stationed in the eternal
Brahman.[14]

☐

1. Chandogya Upanishad 3.4.1
2. Gita 11,32
3. Gita 8.19
4. Isa Upanishad 1.1
5. Srimad Bhagavatam 11,6.15
6. Chandogya Upanishad 3,14,2
7. Gita 2.47
8. Gita 4.23
9. Chandogya Upanishad 6.8.1
10. Chandogya Upanishad 6.13.3
11. Taittiriya Upanishad 3.1
12. Chandogya Upanishad 3.1.1
13. Mundaka Upanishad 3.2.7
14. Chandogya Upanishad 8.13.1

Yoga In Daily Life

SWAMI PRABUDDHANANDA

"Why cannot we hasten the growth of man...? We can. Can we put a limit to the hastenings?... You have no reason to say that this much a man can do and no more. Circumstances can hasten him wonderfully. Can there be any limit until you come to perfection? ...Even this hastening of the growth must be under laws. Suppose we investigate these laws and understand their secrets and apply them to our own needs. It follows that we grow. We hasten our growth, hasten our development. We become perfect even in this life. The utility of this science (Yoga) is to bring out the perfect man and not let him wait and wait for ages just a plaything in the hands of the physical world, like a log of driftwood carried from wave to wave and tossing about in the ocean. This science wants you to be strong: to take the work in your hands instead of leaving it in the hands of nature, and get beyond this little life."[1]

Life implies activity and growth. We constantly evolve in a natural way, but through conscious, intelligent, and steady effort we can accelerate the process. The training and education we receive at home, in schools, and through extensive social contacts expedite this evolution. A new awareness slowly dawns. We begin to perceive, though vaguely, the relationship between ourselves and the group. This opens up new vistas in our consciousness, and on the distant horizon our infinite potentialities unfold before us. We then ascertain additional facts relating to ourselves and the universe that were heretofore unknown to us. These discoveries urge us to probe below the surface of our pragmatic life, and thus we intensify our search for truth. We embark on a lifelong journey seeking peace, security, and complete fulfilment.

Throughout our laborious journey we are impelled to play our part. We constantly struggle to express ourselves and also to explore the world around us in every possible way. We face challenges in diverse areas. Sometimes we win; but often we fight desperately for survival. We contend with many turbulent forces both internal and external along the way. During this struggle with conflicts of interests, clashes of egos, and unrelenting competition, we occasionally become bored, impatient, tired and sometimes we strumble and fall.

In our daily life tensions accumulate, increasing our mental burden. This makes us prone to depression, anger toward others, agressive behaviour, guilt consciousness and self-pity. Our personality contracts under these inner pressures and as a result we are miserable and insecure. Loneliness and lack of support often plague us. We feel we are drifting, lost at sea.

We have to steer our ship through all these tempestuous waters of life in order to reach the safety and security of the shore. Gradually it becomes evident that our search is for something Infinite, permanent, but nevertheless inextricably interwoven with our everyday life. It is essential to learn to utilize every experience, pleasant or unpleasant, big or small to mould our character and expand our consciousness. Every one of these situations should draw us closer to the goal, which according to Vedantic thought is coming face to face with one's own Divine nature, or "to discover the eternal relationship betweeen the eternal Soul and the eternal God."[2] Becoming perfect or going toward God simply means realizing what is already within ourselves. This journey is termed variously as going back home, meeting a long-lost beloved friend, or attaining our own empire. It should be a lively, natural and joyful undertaking.

With resolute hearts we adopt some time-tested techniques in our daily life, and through assiduous practice we ultimately realize the Truth. This realization transforms our life, changes our perspective, and reveals the profound significance of everything we experience. We will then see one indivisible Light shining inside and outside ourselves. We become the embodiment of love, peace, fearlessness and strength. How to accomplish this journey smoothly with conservation of time and energy, and with the maximum benefit to oneself and others is the theme of Yoga.

At the outset the aspirant should be definite about what he is looking for. In order to lay an unshakable foundation in spiritual life, it is indispensable to have a clear idea of the spiritual ideal, and to base this life on the higher realities experienced in the lives of the mystics. These realities are expressed in their teachings and also in other reliable scriptures rooted in eternal verities. Mature reasoning, reflection, and meditation on the ideas contained therein strengthen his spiritual life. They stimulate his mind, remove doubts, and reinforce convictions. This reinforcement of beliefs cannot be emphasized enough. For a long time a firm conviction is one of the main inner supports for the seeker during times of disquietude. This study also protects him from falling in to the clutches of "false prophets", mere social religions, and different types of superstitions.

A sound philosophy, accompanied by love for the Ideal, and one-pointed attention toward its realization facilitate progress along the spiritual path. "Take up one idea. Make that one idea your life; think of it; dream of it; live on that idea. Let the brain, muscles, nerves, every part of your body be full of that idea, and just leave every other idea alone. This is the

way to success, and this is the way great
spiritual giants are produced."[3] In order to
develop this devotion, the seeker needs an
undivided, dispassionate mind endowed with a
lively interest in spiritual realities. A vivid
imagination amplifies his ability to relate these
subtle realities to his workaday life. Until he has
at least a glimpse of the Truth, his only reliable
instruments are a steadfast understanding, the
higher imagination, and trust in the words of
those who have had spiritual experience.
Through continual exercise of this creative
faculty and reassociation of ideas, he will
discover that 'today's imagination becomes
tomorrow's reality.'

The prerequisite of a steady understanding
is the ability to distinguish fact from fancy.
Often Mother Nature tries to hood-wink a
spiritual seeker. Unless he stands firm and
inquires into the nature of the world, he will be a
victim of her tricks. This inquiry requires full use
of all mental faculties. After diligently weighing
the pros and cons and assessing properly all
events he encounters, he should make precise

decisions based on time, place and circumstances. Sri Ramakrishna instructed Sri Sarada Devi, the Holy Mother, to give due consideration to all situations and then adjust her behaviour according to the need of the moment. However, the natural inclination in most cases is to forge ahead when things are amiable and advantageous and to procrastinate or avoid, when things are complicated or troublesome. How to follow Sri Ramakrishna's trenchant advice? Whether the occasion is agreeable or disagreeable one should pause briefly before acting. The formula is: pause, reflect, feel the ground,—and then proceed. In this way circumspection enables the seeker to recognize gradually that all phenomena have only temporary values. In order to escape Mother Nature's spell and reclaim his lost heritage of innate freedom and bliss, he has to scrutinize carefully and develop a correct attitude toward the relative universe. Furthermore, based on this attitude he should designate the appropriateness of all pursuits, such as building up a career, and acquisition of knowledge and wealth, as well as human relationships, events, and other things of the world, and consonantly choose his course of action.

Through careful application of the above formula, he observes the passing nature of all phenomena, and mercilessly inquires into common sense experiences. That is to say, he asks himself: what is the meaning of all these experiences, what do I expect to gain from them, how long will they last, and what is their worth? Through such critical inquiry he discovers why his energies are ordinarily exhausted, his resources drained, and he is left feeling empty inside. He finds out, "Bliss is to be found only in the Infinite, never in the finite."[4] When various temptations rear their heads and try to drag him into false and irrelevant ways of thinking and acting, he should be able to say with conviction: "I don't see anything worthwhile or meaningful here." Like the proverbial swan, he needs to separate water from milk.

A related way of distinguishing fact from fancy is to try to perceive the world objectively—as it actually is and not what one wishes it to be. Man has the faculty of standing aside and viewing himself, others, and all happenings in life as a spectator. He can gaze calmly at them and allow them to pass. This witness-consciousness is the core of his being, and is in essence ever pure, ever free, and ever blessed. A spiritual seeker should continuously assert this fact that his real being is one, full of bliss, and immortal. Once in a conversation Swami Vivekananda had with Miss Josephine MacLeod he said, "Incidentally you are a woman, incidentally you are an American, but you are always a child of God."[5] The seeker thinks: If I am a pure blissful child of God, then all others are also children of God. We are all One, Indivisible Satchidananda. How can there be any fear, insecurity or inane competition for me once this false individuality is subdued and transcended? Love is the expression of Oneness. This fact is beautifully exemplified in the *Brhadaranyaka Upanishad* teaching that all beings are loved, not for their own sake, but because of the Self present in them.

Love is central to man's existence. "Who would have lived and breathed, had not this sky of bliss existed?"[6] Emotions are a source of tremendous power. Therefore, cultivation of the heart is salient in spiritual life. Swamiji said, "If there is conflict between the intellect and the heart, always follow the heart."[7] To incorporate Swamiji's suggestion properly, the aspirant has to undergo a step-by-step process of emotional refinement. Further, as Swamiji indicates, "the various feelings in the human heart are not wrong in themselves; only they have to be carefully controlled and given a higher direction, until they attain the very highest condition of excellence."[8] So this process involves intensifying, purifying, and redirecting these inner forces. Such disciplines as self-control, truthfulness, kindness toward all beings, study of religious texts, etc., have been emphasized by all religious traditions with this aim in view. A strong, yet flexible, character is the mainstay in spiritual life. In Holy Mother's language, 'God is purity itself and cannot be realized without the practice of control of the body and mind.'"[9] The intelligent aspirant discerns this, and with caution and patience treads the path chalked out by the past magnanimous spiritual luminaries. He voluntarily restrains himself and strives to imbibe their teachings in this regard.

Cautious
Courteous
Cooperative.

Conscientious performance of duty is one of the significant instructions given to the seeker for the efficient channeling of his energy in a socially beneficial way. A whole-hearted and cheerful commitment to the duties and responsibilities connected with his station in life is of prime importance. As mentioned previously, in order to expand his consciousness, the seeker has to take one step at a time. If he shirks his responsibilities, he will have to learn later through bitter experience. There is no shortcut in this growing process. He must continue with the work on hand until higher duty calls, and then only he will find, "The only true duty is to be unattached and to work as free beings, to give up all work unto God." [10] Apart from making the group life smooth and rewarding, this commitment helps him to control, and eventually outgrow, his impulses, obsessions, and prejudices, and brings him inner relief and satisfaction. How to perform one's duties? Just as while driving in rush hour traffic, he has to be cautious, courteous, and cooperative with other drivers to reach his destination safely, similarly, he has to coordinate his life and activities with others and build up a healthy ego which is essential for the practice of Yoga. After all, the aim of Yoga is to ripen the ego and gradually to shift from ego-centredness to God-centeredness. 'I' becomes 'we', 'we' becomes 'all'. This expansion brings peace and freedom. A student wrote to his teacher asking for his advice on acquiring peace of mind. The wise teacher replied, "Do you know how many times you have used the word 'I' in your letter? Forty-eight times! How can you have peace of mind?" Swamiji says, "Unselfishness is God."[11]

Simultaneous with this strengthening of our moral fibre and purification of heart, we should develop deep love and respect for our great spiritual teachers because it is they who compassionately inspire us to seek first the Kingdom of God. Once in response to the question, "How can one get devotion?" Mahapurushji Maharaj, Swami Shivananda, replied, "Holy company." And then added, "The holy men lead one to god."[12] The living touch of illumined souls infuses an immediate sense of the Divine. "Five minutes in their presence will change a whole life."[13] The environment plays a prominent part in the healthy growth of spirituality. In a subtle way we are influenced by the mental and physical atmosphere that we are immersed in daily. The need for holy company to counteract these influences is paramount. The lives and teachings of these teachers subdue the onrushing worldly tendencies and awaken the hidden spiritual inclinations.

Let us unreservedly expose ourselves to their teachings and turn to them for guidance. The first instruction concerns daily Japa, prayer, and meditation. With the help of a graphic imagination, penetrating thought, and deep feeling let us fill ourselves with the Presence of God who is the Reality of everything, and who is all-pervading like the warp and woof of a cloth. He is also the indwelling Spirit who is our very essence, the driving force, and the support. He also responds to prayers with compassion and love. The same Infinite Spirit comes down, as it were, as Divine Incarnation to help one and all through guidance, inspiration, and Divine wisdom which dispels all fear and ignorance.

Repetition of the Divine Name, if done with a concentrated mind and warmth of feeling, will help us to sustain the remembrance of Him. When the Name penetrates the inner recesses of the heart, it will not only lead to deep meditation, but will also surface when needed during times of stress or struggles with undesirable thoughts or moods. "As wind removes a cloud, so does the name of God disperse the cloud of worldliness."[14] Let us pray fervently from the bottom of our heart for purity, guidance, and strength for ourselves, and for the good of others. The power of prayer awakens one's spiritual consciousness and also imperceptibly helps others. "When you pray, pray with all your heart and soul. When you meditate, try to be one with God, to have the consciousness of unity and identity. One should by all means practise like this."[15] This effort to dive deeper into oneself makes the mind comparatively transparent and creates a spiritual mood.

Equipped with this mood and having a spiritual attitude in the background, we should do all the daily activities trying to remain in that state by adopting diverse methods as Brother

Lawerence did. He said, "The time of business does not with me differ from the time of prayer,"[16] and in another place, "Our sanctification did not depend upon changing our works, but in doing that for God's sake which we commonly do for our own."[17] And in Swamiji's words, "The daily necessary thoughts can all be thoughts through God. Eat to Him, drink to Him, sleep to Him, talk about Him to others, see Him in all."[18]

"Be steadfast in Yoga and perform actions."[19] To practise this effectively the following Yoga kit is recommended: Plan the day and your life always bearing in mind that there is a Higher Power who can supersede or upset your plans any time. When you meet people cover them with God, and treat them appropriately according to each one's need. Consider work as God. It is God's work you are doing as His instrument and merely for His pleasure. As the work progresses, offer it "to Him from whom everything has originated and by whom everything is pervaded."[20] When work flows smoothly, offer it to Him with a greatful heart as you offer a fragrant, full-blown flower at His feet. If there is trouble, tension, or heart-ache while working, dedicate that also to Him. Let Him enjoy a "hot dish" occasionally! During dry periods and "dark nights" remember repeatedly that God is with you as your own Self, whether you are aware of it or not. When guilt-consciousness stings, say, "Good or bad, I'm a child of the Mother." When you feel lonely or let down, say with feeling and conviction, "Thou art my All in All, O Lord!" When a problem or a doubt arises, first refer it to Him and pray for light and guidance, and then to whatever is humanly possible for solving it. If the Lord delays response, create a tremendous commotion with Him. When some occasions try to unnerve you, take refuge in Him and face them boldly. We are "all children of Immortal Bliss."[21] Let humour spice and lighten our lives. A teacher once said, "We need the skin of a rhinoceros and a sense of humour." Hum a song or a hymn whenever convenient. Intersperse the activities of your day with silent repetition of the name of God. Now and then think you are like the sky, vast, pure, and unattached to everything, and the events of this world are passing like the clouds. At the completion of a job dedicate the results to Him. Just as an accountant closes his books at the end of the day, or a cashier deposits money in the bank and then feels relieved of the responsibility, in a similar way free yourself from the ego burden. When you rest, feel that you are lying in the lap of the Infinite Spirit as a bird in its nest. This kind of practice enables one to have a spiritual undercurrent at all times and under all circumstances.

To sum up, let us practice Yoga as the mood and need come. We have certain guidelines for disciplines, but in and through those we should move freely. Let us study the different Yogas - Jnana, Bhakti, Karma, and Raja - separately and understand them clearly, but always remember in daily life they blend together. The human mind does not function compartmentally. So it is advisable to practise them simultaneously, making full use of all the faculties of the mind intelligently. Let us not become onesided by trying to squeeze ourselves into this or that mould due to pride, false humility, or any other reason. Our working ideal is to be harmoniously balanced. Here the two vital points for us to note

are: (1) We should practise Yoga
systematically by purifying and strengthening
our intellect, emotions and will. (2) We should
dive deep and become absorbed in whatever
practice we are engaged in, and not
over-emphasize its external form. From the
beginning of our spiritual life let us focus our
attention on the actual contact with the Supreme
Spirit who is the goal of our life.

In this way if we sedulously introduce the
spiritual element in all areas of life, the
corresponding results are bound to come
according to the law of Karma: "As we sow, so
we reap." Moreover, the fountain of the Lord's
unconditioned grace is perpetually overflowing.
Mahapurushji Maharaj once told some one that
resignation to God and reliance on His grace
were all in all. "If one goes ten steps to God, God
comes a hundred steps to receive him."
Furthermore, to act as a loving guide and
companion, the Supreme Spirit manifests
Himself as the Divine Incarnation. If we take
refuge in Him, He will become the Pilot to steer
our ship of spiritual life. Through His power and
love our journey is quickened, and very soon our

ship reaches the other shore. In this cosmic scheme where so much help is available, can there by any doubt about reaching perfection here and now in this very life? □

---

1 CW of Swami Vivekananda, 1970 ed., 2:9

2 Ibid, 3:4

3 ibid, 1:177

4 Chandogya Upanishad, Chapter 7, v.23, Madras Math, 1956 ed.

5 Reminiscences of Swami Vivekananda, Advaita Ashrama, 1961 ed, page 236

6 Taittiriya Upanishad, Chapter 2, Lesson 7, Madras Math, 1965 ed.

7 CW of Swami Vivekananda, 1965 ed. 1:412

8 Ibid, 3:78

9 Swami Nikhilananda, Holy Mother, 1962 ed., page 223

10 CW of Swami Vivekananda, 1965 ed. 1:103

11 Ibid, 1:87

12 For Seekers of God, Advaita Ashrama, 1972 ed., Page 218

13 Teachings of Swami Vivekananda, Advaita
    Ashrama, 1953 ed, page 9

14 Swami Nikhilananda, Holy Mother, 1962
    ed., page 220

15 For Seekers of God, Advaita Ashrama,
    1972 ed; page 55

16 The Practice of the Presence of God,
    Fleming H. Revell Co., 1970 ed. page 29

17 Ibid, p 23

18 CW of Swami Vivekananda, 1969 ed., 7:9

19 Srimad Bhagavad Gita, Chapter 2, v.48,
    Advaita Ashrama, 1966 ed.

20 Ibid, 18:46

21 Svetasvataropanishad, Chapter 2, v.5,
    Madras Math. 1943 ed.

Yoga And Tantra

S. SHANKARANARAYANAN

If at all there is a branch of knowledge
which is much maligned and much
misunderstood, it is the Tantra Sastra. All the
misunderstanding stems from the
non-understanding of the subject. Perhaps the
Sastra itself has to be blamed. Its principles are
not intelligible to the common man and its
practices are heavily veiled in secrecy. Added
to that, the Sastra frowns on the unbeliever with
its strictures, confounds the critic with its
misleading nomenclature, baffles the uninitiate
with its codes and conundrums and laughs at the
sceptic with its down-to-earth approach.

It is usual amongst scholars, to classify the
evolution of Hindu religion, as beginning with
the Vedas, followed by the Upanishads and
then later by the Puranas and Tantra Sastra.
The Hindu religion as it is practised in this
country today is based on the Puranas and
Tantras. From this it has been concluded that

the Tantra is a later development in Hindu religious thought and its practices are of recent origin.

But this is against the Indian tradition itself. Throughout the ages, the Veda has been considered as a revealed scripture, not written by any human hand, that which has come down, *agama*. Later when the Tantra Sastra became available in a codified form no human authorship was ascribed to it. It was also considered as a revealed scripture and the appellation *agama* was used in its case as well. Afterwards to make a distinction, the Veda began to be known as *nigama*, the Tantra was called *agama*. Later on that part of the Tantra Sastra which deals with the construction of temples and temple worship has come to be known as *agama*.

Just as we cannot say that Yoga was not known in India before Patanjali wrote his Yoga aphorisms. We cannot conclude that practice of Tantra was not prevalent in ancient India before the Tantric texts in codified form appeared in the fourteenth century. In fact the Tantra should have been known and widely practised in India from very early times.

The word Tantra is derived from the Sanskrit root *tan* to spread, to elaborate in detail. Therefore, Tantra has come to mean any elaboration, a detailed act, *modus operandi*, a technique of doing things. Popularly the Tantric act represents a rite, a ritual and the Tantra has been acclaimed as a pragmatic science.

The Tantra does not, as is imagined by many, run counter to the spirit of the Veda. On the other hand it holds the Veda in high reverence. It embodies in its teaching the knowledge of the Veda, the wisdom of the Upanishads and the Yoga tradition of the country in a grand synthesis.

"The Synthesis is a living whole in which every element of value is preserved and falls into its just position and proportion—all together making quite a new and developing system which embraces the entire life in its sweep, the man in individual and man in the aggregate, man the thinker and the doer, man the soul. This synthesis of the Tantra is in fact more comprehensive than the synthesis of the

Gita and in a sense more in consonance with Intention in life!"*

In this Synthesis, four famous parts *pada* go to make up the whole—the *Jnana pada,* the *Yoga Pada,* the *Kriya pada* and the *Charya pada.* The *Jnana pada* supplies the metaphysical base. The esoteric message of the Veda coupled with the psychology of the Sankhyas and the thought of the Upanishads form the philosophical basis of the Tantra. The Supreme is One and All is He; the universe is a manifestation of His Sakti. The *Yoga pada* deals with the *yogic* discipline handed over traditionally from the Master to the disciple. Jnana Yoga, Bhakti Yoga, Kundalini Yoga, and the unique contribution of the Tantra Sastra to the esoteric science, Mantra Yoga are diligently employed, as appropriate, according to the instruction of the Master. The *Kriya pada* is the heart of the Tantra Sastra. It deals with the practice,. the *modus operandi* of the Sadhana. It stresses on external ceremonies, ritual and worship in order to awaken the naturally extrovert consciousness of man to the reality of an Inner Presence. The *Charya pada* lays down the code of conduct, how the ideal individual, the Tantric Yogi, should conduct himself in the world for the general welfare of the society in which he lives.

The Tantras are generally classified as Saiva, Vaishnava and Sakta according as the paramount God worshipped is Siva, Vishnu or Sakti. Sakta Tantras are more comprehensive in nature and their teaching is available for all those who aspire, irrespective of caste, clime or creed.

The Upanishads describe the *modus operandi* of creation in three ways: He the Lord desired that he should become the Many *so' kamayata*. That one saw *tadaikshata*. He consciously energised himself *sa tapo' tapyata*. These are the three poises of the creative Godhead, the release *Srshti* of his Force Sakti as creation. Thus creation is the resultant of Sakti in the form of *iccha* desire, will, *jnana* perception, knowledge and *kriya* action, energy. The world is a gradual evolution of Sakti, the progressive unfoldment of God Power, a continuous development, an incessant blossoming of the Bliss and Beauty of the

Divine. The world is no myth, no illusion. It is as real as the Reality which created it. The world is *Maya* in the sense that it is measured out of the immeasurable One and the great measurer Mahamaya is Sakti Herself. In the Tantric path, nothing is rejected, nothing is negated. To attain something you need not leave something else. To be engrossed in the world, indifferent to the Call of the Spirit is not what is sought for. To be entrenched in the Spirit indifferent to the clamouring humanity and its needs is also not what is aimed at. Man is of the Earth and Heaven, matter and spirit. He cannot deny his parentage either from the one or from the other. Both liberation and enjoyment, Mukti and Bhwkti, are the aims. The Tantra does not shun or reject manifested Nature and its difficulties. It confronts them, seizes and conquers.

One of the main discoveries of the Tantra is that whatever is in the macrocosm *anda* is in the microcosm *pinda*. The different planes from where the cosmic functions come into play have their correspondence in the beings that are in creation. In us, there are different planes and parts, quite distinct, at the same time coordinating into a harmonious unit of the whole being. These planes are governed by conscious centres and sources of the dynamic powers of the being which act as focal points for the consciousness to operate. These centres, picturesquely known as *cakras,* wheels of power, or *padmas* lotuses, ready to unfold, are situated in our subtle body and are arranged in an ascending series from the lowest physical to the highest mind centre and spiritual centre called the thousand-petalled lotus where ascending Nature, the Serpent-power of the Tantrics, meets the Brahman and is liberated into the Divine Being. The force of Nature, the Sakti lying coiled or asleep in the lowest centre Muladhara, the Kundalini Sakti when awakened through Yoga uncoils herself and begins to rise upward like a fiery serpent until she meets Siva, the Brahman in the head centre. The human being is like an ice-berg. Only a very small portion of his personality is visible on the surface. Infinite are his potentialities and the Tantra Sastra aids him in his self-blossoming.

Let us now deal with the three cardinal concepts of the Tantra.

First is the concept of the Deity, *devata*.
The Tantra recognises the one Supreme Deity
presiding over everything as the Highest, at the
same time admitting the existence of various
Gods and Goddesses. "The sages of the Tantra
do not see any inconsistency in the position, for
they recognise that this creation is not a unitary
system but a gradation of worlds spread over a
rising tier of consciousness and· planes. The
various Gods and Goddesses are higher beings,
powers and entities deriving their authority
from the Supreme to take their part and act or
preside over their spheres or domain. There is
a regular heirarchy of Gods, some of whom are
far above the highest heavens of human reach.
But there are also Gods and Goddesses closer
to the human level. They are more readily
accessible to those who aspire to them and in
some cases the seeker on the Tantric path looks
to the aid and lead of these deities in his effort.
They are endowed with capacities and powers
beyond normal human possibility, but they are
not all for that reason divine in nature. There
are higher and lower classes of them, *uccha* and
kshudra devatas!"* The *kshudra devatas* are

*   Sri Kapali Sastriar in *Sidelights on Tantra.*

readily-responding entities in the subtle world, a low order of deities who gratify the aspirant with petty gifts, lull him into a false sense of progress and security and finally bring his ruin. The *uccha devatas* are benevolent deities who take the seeker on the path steadily and safely and ultimately do him the utmost good. Each God is distinct, and can be distinguished by his particular form, ornaments, weapons and retinue.

The second concept which is unique to the Tantra is the Mantra. The quickest way to have a realisation of the Deity is through its Mantra. Mantra is not a mere arrangement of letters. When the Transcendent Brahman desires to manifest out of its own volition, there is a stir, a throb *spanda* which starts a series of vibrations. These take the form of sound *nada* which is the origin of the whole creation. Each deity has its own *nada*, lines of vibration, in the high supernal. The Rishi hears in his occult audition the characteristic *nada* and when it is transmitted in the articulate tongue, it becomes the Mantra. The Mantra enshrines the Deity and reveals the Deity to the earnest seeker. The Mantra is not, as popularly held, a means to contact the Deity. It is the Deity itself. It is the sound-body of the Deity having a remarkable correlation with the body of the Deity that is contemplated in Dhyana.

The third concept is the grand concept of the Guru. If the Mantra is the sound-body of the Deity, who can reveal the Mantra except the Deity itself? Ultimately it is the Deity that leads the devotee to itself. But all are not in a position to get the direct guidance from the Deity. Certain rare souls who come to earth as already prepared or perfected beings need no outside help. They rely on their inner voice, on the God within them, and advance very rapidly. But for all the others the Deity acts through a human agency, the Guru. Knowledge is handed over without a break by means of initiation. And for this perpetual movement, continuous guidance, the Tantra gives the name, *augha,* flood or current. The Aughas are three in number, Divyaugha, Siddhaugha and Manavaugha, the divine guides, the accomplished or semi-divine companions on the way and the mortal mentors. If man is ready, he is caught in this current and led by the current without any effort. When the seeker is earnest, the Guru appears on the scene to guide him. So the Guru is not a mere human being. To mistake him as such is a sure way to spiritual downfall. He is the delegated power of the God-head on earth and to the disciple he is God Himself. If a Mantra has to be effective, it has to be initiated through a Guru.

The secret of Sadhana is to realise the unity of oneself with the Guru, Devata and Mantra *gurudevata manunam aikyam.*

In the path of the Tantra, man is not branded as a sinner; his numerous failings are not looked down upon with contempt and scorn. If man is imperfect, it is because Sakti in him has not come into full play. He need not reject any part of his being, need not be ashamed of himself. The very things that degrade a man are taken up for accomplishing the upward climb. *Yaireva patanam nrnam siddhis taireva codita.* The Tantra recognises man primarily as a *pasu,* the inert Tamasic, unregenerate being with animal instincts predominant. Worship is prescribed for such a common man and by the dint of worship itself,

he flowers into the Rajasic man, full of vigour
and activity, the hero-warrior *vira* who
proceeds on the path with undaunted will and is
ready to take Heaven by storm. Then the *vira*
evolves into a *divya* the Godman who with his
Sattvic maturity and silent power carries on his
calm brow the burden of the Gods. Thus the
Tantra recognises the competency, *adhikari
bheda* of the individual and it helps him in his
gradual evolution.

Basing on the classification of
competency, the Tantra has devised two main
paths to reach the goal—the *vama Marga* and
the *Dakshina Marga*, the Left Hand and the
Right Hand Paths, or more correctly the Way of
Delight and the Way of Knowledge. From early
times both the paths have been treated with
equal respect, though later on Vama Marga fell
into disrepute. This is not little due to the
ignorance of the votaries of Vama Marga who
did not understand the symbolic meaning and
spiritual significance of the external sensory
objects with which they have to conduct
worship.

What are these objects? These are indicated in code as the *Pancha Makaras,* five 'M's and they have been the main cause of all the bad name for the Tantra Sastra. These are Madhu, Matsya, Mamsa, Mudra and Maithuna-wine, fish, flesh, which constitute food—all activity sealed, *mudra* which is sleep and Maithuna, sex. Thus these five words beginning with 'M' denote food, sleep and sex to which all human beings are subjected. Man can never be free unless he is free from the rule of food, sleep and sex. So an aspirant has to eschew these in favour of the Divine. He has to make an offering of all these to the Divine. If a person is not using *madhu* wine in his normal life, the Tantra does not ask him to procure it as an offering for worship. For him *madhu* has an inner meaning, it may be the honey, the sweetness in things, the *rasa* the delectable relish, the Ananda of life. Like that every word in this category has an inner meaning and spiritual significance. And if this is not known, verily the Tantric practice becomes as dangerous as riding on a tiger's back, *vyaghra prishthadhirohanam,* as perilous as walking on a razor's edge, *asidhara vratam.*

We owe not a little to the works of spiritual stalwarts like Sri Bhaskararaya for the correct appreciation and understanding of the principles and practice of the Tantras. In our own times, the works of Sir John Woodroffe, alias Arthur Avalon, the writings of Sri Aurobindo on the subject, the thoughts of Sri Kavyakantha Vasishtha Ganapati Muni expressed in his *magnum opus* 'Uma Sahasram' and other works like 'Mahavidyadi Sutras' and the flood of Light thrown by Sri Kapali Sastriar in his succinct articles—all have helped to remove the prejudice in the popular minds about Tantra Sastra, restoring it to its place of pristine purity.

Last but not the least, the saga of Sadhana practised by the Master, Sri Ramakrishna Paramahamsa with Bhairavi Brahmani in the beginning of this century stands eloquent testimony to the eternal values and infallible methods of Tantra Sastra.

The Tantra Sastra is catholic in its approach and its teachings are available to all irrespective of caste, creed or sex. The special place of honour it gives to woman is unique. In the Tantra, more than the companion, mate and life-partner of man, the Woman is his creator and the creator of everything. She is the Mother.

> *Ya devi sarvabhuteshu matrurupena*
> *samsthita*
> *Namastasyai namastasyai namastasyai*
> *namo namah.*

□

Yoga In Srimad Bhagavata

SWAMI SIDDHINATHANANDA

Words are of three kinds: 1) those with conventional or traditional meanings, irrespective of their root-meanings. They are called Roodha: e.g. *gau* (cow) 2) Those with derivational or etymological meanings. They are called Yaugika e.g. *sukhada* (Pleasure-giving) 3) Those with etymological meaning and at the same time confined to a conventional meaning. They are called Yogaroodha: e.g. *pankaja* (mudborn lotus).

The word Yoga has a wide variety of connotations ranging from absorption in the Ultimate Spirit to an Ayurvedic recipe, all retaining the etymological affinity in varying nuances. Thus the word Yoga has a wide orbit in the Yougika group. It has also a Yogaroodha connotation. In common parlance, Yoga means the Yoga system of philosophy propounded by Patanjali.

Sankhya, Yoga, Nyaya, Vaiseshika, Purva Mimamsa, Uttara Mimamsa are the six orthodox systems of Indian philosophy. Of these, Yoga alone has the unique distinction of being accepted as a practical spiritual science while the others are mostly speculative in character. Though Mimamsa has a practical side, its fruits are available only in the next world, while the fruits of Yoga are available here and now. Its technique has been adapted and adopted by most of philosophic and spiritual traditions of India. Thus the scope of Yoga has widened immensely. At present, it has crossed the bounds of Hinduism and has been welcomed by other faiths as well, especially by Christianity. Under the inspiration of indigenisation adopted by the Catholic Church, many Indian Christians have taken to the Yogic modes of meditation. Transcendental meditation has made itself at home abroad also. It may also be added inter-alia that in its adventures abroad Yoga has acquired some bad odour in certain parts of Europe.

At a Hindu-Christian Dialogue held in June last at Rajpur near Dehra Dun under the World

Council of Churches, there was a discussion about the mutual sharing of traditions. Yoga and meditation were recommended. When Yoga was mentioned, a Professor of Theology from Denmark got up and stoutly opposed it. He said Yoga is a stinking word in many parts of Europe and if the word is used without sufficient safeguards, the whole proceedings would be suspect in the eyes of many in Europe and no decent man will touch it with even a barge-pole. The reason was that there are some Indian 'Yogins' roaming about in some parts of Europe preaching and practising free sex in the name of Yoga. The social situation in some Scandinavian and other European countries seem to be congenial for such stuff and some unscrupulous people are dragging down the fair name of Yoga. Yoga also has its unlucky stars.

Yoga being a psychological path to perfection, it is universal in its appeal. Though it is primarily a spiritual path, it owes its popularity more to its miracle-working side effect than to its main purpose. Its potential to provide physical well-being also contributes to its popular appeal. But to use it for any goal

other than spiritual is a misuse. Patanjali
intended it to be a straight path to reveal the soul
in its pristine purity devoid of all mental
distractions and limitations.

Of the eight steps of Patanjali's Ashtanga
Yoga, the first two, Yama and Niyama are
preliminary steps to attain purity of mind and
body. These have been adopted by all systems
and hence the Ashtanga Yoga is sometimes
referred to as Shadanga Yoga, the Yoga with six
steps. The main thrust of the Yogic method is
negative in that it consists of negating the
distracting ideations of the mind. When the sky
is clear, the sun shines in its own glory. But the
negative process is arduous and tortuous. So
Patanjali provides for meditation on a pure
heart, a flame, God or anything sublime.

Contemplation is the content of Yoga,
meditation is the means and concentration, the
core. By providing for fixing the mind on God
or any sublime object, Patanjali has opened the
gate of Yoga to one and all. It is common
experience that the mind gets concentrated on
anything that is to its liking. Give it something
enchanting and it gets attracted. This is a

positive approach and that is the method the
path of devotion has adopted. It is in this
context that we can speak of Yoga in Srimad
Bhagavata.

Ordinarily we speak of four Yogas, the
royal roads to Reality, viz., Jnana, Bhakti, Raja
and Karma Yogas. Strangely enough, the
Bhagavata does not recognise Rajayoga as an
independent path. It speaks of only three. Sri
Krishna says to Uddhava: 'I have propounded
three Yogas for the welfare of mankind. They
are Jnana, Karma and Bhakti and there is none
other anywhere. Jnana Yoga for those who are
disillusioned with the world and have given up
Karma; Karmayoga for those who hanker after
worldly pleasures and are attached to Karma;
and Bhaktiyoga for those who happen to hear
about Me and My sports and are attracted by
them, yet are not totally free from worldly
pursuits nor are very much attached to them.'
(Bh. II.10. 6,7,8)

Though the Bhagavata does not accord an
independent status to Patanjali's Yoga, it
recommends and incorporates all its limbs in
the practice of meditation. Yama, Niyama,

Asana, Pranayama and the whole host are there, may be in a slightly modified form. (Vide Bhag. 11.14.32-35; and 11.19.33-35).

Having appropriated its methodology, why did the Bhagavata not give Yoga its due? The Yoga system is an offshoot of Sankhya and is complementary to it. Original Sankhya had no place for God and that was found to be a drawback. In order to remove that want, Yoga was evolved with a place for God, however circumscribed though. Kapila was the initial propounder of Sankhya system. The Bhagavata has devoted an important section for Kapila and his philosophy. Here Kapila's system is completely theistic and therefore, there was no need for a separate system of Yoga. Hence the Bhagavata's silence about Yoga as a separate path.

Now of the three Yogas acknowledged by the Bhagavata, which one holds the pride of place? Uddhava asked Krishna: 'Lord, wise men have propounded many a path for the good of man. Is any of them good enough or is there any surpassing all?' (Bh. 11.14.1). In reply Krishna says: 'I am attainable by Bhakti alone;

devotion to Me purifies even the born sinner'
(Bh. 11,14.21).

Vyasa has propounded the path of Jnana in
the Brahmasutras and that of Karma in the
Bhagavad Gita. The Bhagavata was composed
with the express intention of singing the glories
of the path of Bhakti. Though all the paths find
a place in the epic, the pride of place is given to
Bhakti. Indeed, the Bhagavata is the greatest
scripture of the Bhakti-path.

Love of God is devotion. It has various
gradations depending on the degree of the love
of God. Innumerable types of devotion are
depicted in the great epic. Sages like Suka and
Narada, kings like Prithu and Ambarisha, boys
like Dhruva and Prahlada, women like Kunti,
Devahuti and the Gopis, Asuras like Vritra and
Hiranyakasipu indeed the Asuras are also
devotees in disguise — animals like the
elephant and the crocodile and several others
are representatives of devotion in its various
dimensions. Each is unique, grand and glorious.

Which of these is relevant for us in the
context of Yoga? We shall confine ourselves to

Devahuti and the instruction she received from her gifted son. Of all the women that had the good fortune to be mothers of incarnations, Devahuti stands alone in that only she sought spiritual enlightenment from her godly son, Kapila. The process that Patanjali teaches is mainly a negative one. It demands the arrestment of mental modifications. Here in this shadowy chase, both the hound and the hare are the mind. So it often turns out to be a wild goose chase. True, Patanjali prescribes a course of positive approach also. It is this positive part of Yoga that Kapila of the Bhagavata incorporates into his devotional Yoga. When the mind dwells on a charming divine form, it gets infused and suffused by divinity with the result that the mind gets dissolved in the divine and that is a more practical approach than the other. This is the Yoga that Kapila in the Bhagavata imparts to his mother Devahuti.

Devahuti, the daughter of the first Manu, was married to Kardama. They had nine daughters and one son. The son was a partial manifestation of Vishnu and was known as

Kapila. Soon after the birth of the son, Kardama left home and became a wandering monk. Kapila, was the first philosopher. He came down to impart spiritual wisdom to mankind. Devahuti who knew the divine greatness of her son, one day approached him and said: 'Lord, I am fed up with sense pleasures. The more they are is pursued the more they lead one to darkness. By God's grace, I have got you who will lead me out of this impenetrable darkness. Deign to rescue me from the clutches of this identification with the body. I take refuge in you. You are the best one to save bound souls. Please instruct me in the right knowledge of the Self and the non-Self.'

On hearing this noble aspiration of his mother, Kapila said with a smile: 'Spiritual at-one-ment attained as a result of mental concentration is, in my opinion, the way for man to obtain eternal good. By such concentration there will be a total cessation of both pleasure and pain. O Noble One, I will tell you that Yoga with all its limbs which I imparted to the eager Rishis of yore. I think the mind is at the root of both bondage and freedom. The mind that dwells on the world leads to bondage and the mind that is drawn to the soul leads to freedom.'

The mind can make a heaven of hell or a hell of heaven. Elsewhere the Bhagavata says that all spiritual disciplines are meant to bring the mind under control. It is no easy job. It is like controlling the wind, complains Arjuna. Krishna concedes the point, but assures Arjuna that by continued, constant attempt and detachment it is possible to control the mind. If the practice is sustained, ultimate victory is assured by all spiritual teachers.

Its *modus operandi* is being described by Kapila: 'When the mind becomes pure, having been rid of the stains of lust and greed born of identification with the body, and becomes unaffected by pain or pleasure, then the aspirant with a mind infused with detachment, wisdom and devotion will realise the soul shining in its own glory without any taint of the world — the soul that is hard to comprehend, unlimited by time or space and the eternal witness of the phenomenal panorama. Then the Prakriti is absolutely powerless against such a soul.'

The identification of the soul with the body is the root-cause of bondage. From that original sin flow lust, greed and a whole host of the evil brood. The Gordian knot has to be cut at some point. Where to begin? When the soul feels the oppression of the sense-world troublesome, cry a halt, detach the mind from it. But the mind cannot remain in a vacuum. It has to be supplied with something positive, or it will slide back into its old rut. So, fill it with spiritual wisdom gleaned from the scriptures and spiritual masters and soak it with devotion to God. The feet of God are its safest sanctuary. Once the mind has been able to feel the supreme pleasure and blessedness of the divine, the world and its charms cannot lure it any more. Prakriti's play is done and the soul shines in its pristine glory.

This is a culmination that is attained only as a result of long and sustained Sadhana. Kapila indicates the easiest and safest path — this pilgrimage of the soul: 'There is no other path equal to the path of devotion to God, the soul of all, to lead man to eternal blessedness.'

The path of Knowledge is an uphill task all through and if one loses his ground, one is likely to land in atheism. The path of Karma is ultimately inadequate in that it is unable to confer freedom upon the agent. Yoga bereft of Bhakti may degenerate into miracle-mongering. The path of Bhakti, on the other hand is smooth, safe, secure and sweet throughout — in the beginning, in the middle and in the end. Narada also says in his aphorisms on devotion that Bhakti is superior to Karma, Jnana and Yoga. Vyasa affirms the same in several passages in the Bhagavata.

How to obtain and retain Bhakti? Kapila continues: 'The wise consider attachment to worldly things as the relentless fetter of man; the same attachment directed to godly man is an open door to heaven.'

The same mental energy directed worldward binds and directed Godward releases. One cannot tackle the mind by open confrontation; its course has to be tactfully directed towards the good. The company of devotees is a great safeguard for the beginner. It is like the fence for a sapling. Those established in the path find happiness only in the company of devotees. If an elephant after washing is left to itself, it will soon soil itself with mud and dust; but if it is kept in a clean shed after washing, it will remain clean. The company of devotees is the safe shed for the new entrant into the path.

How to recognise a godly man whose company is to be sought and cultivated? Here are the characteristics by which one may recognise such people: 'They will be forbearing and kind to all; they are friendly to all and inimical to none. They bear illwill to no one. They will be calm and composed and nobility will be their natural endowment. They are devoted to Me to the exclusion of every other thought; they will have given up every other occupation for My sake and they will have forsaken their kith and kin for Me. They will always be engaged in hearing and narrating the sacred stories of Mine. No kind of misery or grief will assail those whose minds are riveted on Me. These people, O Noble Lady, who are free from all worldly taints, are the truly good and noble ones. One should earnestly wish for their company, for their company redeems one from the evil arising out of other worldly bonds.' (Bh. 3.25 1-25)

Holy company is the sine qua non for spiritual aspirants of all persuasions. The Bhagavata calls it an invaluable treasure.

Kapila continued to extol the glories of good company and indicated the ways and means of cultivating Bhakti. He instructed Devahuti in the path of Sankhya that leads to devotion. When Purusha realises from experience that Prakriti is not worth associating with, she turns away from him, and he shines in his native glory. Dream works havoc to the dreamer; it can do nothing when one is awake. Similarly, Prakriti, although the cause of misery for the ignorant, is quite harmless to one whose mind is fixed on God. When one is not attracted by the miracles accruing from the practice of Yoga, then the aspirant attains to the ultimate goal of life where the roar of Yama's guffaw will no more be heard.

Kapila said: 'O Royal Lady, I will tell you now the scope and sign of Yoga with a support whereby the mind rid of its dross turns to the path of truth.'

Kapila is here expounding the *sabija* Yoga, Yoga with a support in contradistinction to the negation of mental ripples advised by Patanjali. This is the distinctive feature of Yoga as adumbrated in the Bhagavata. The various steps of Yoga are being detailed: 'Do your prescribed duty as far as possible; avoid all forbidden acts. Be content with what chance brings. Serve the wise; keep away from worldly pursuits. Be intent on attaining liberation. Live on pure food in restricted quantity. Stay in a secure and solitary place always. Harm no one in any manner. Be devoted to truth. Covet not other's property. Accept minimum things, just enough to keep the body going. Avoid carnal cravings; keep the body, senses and mind under control. Keep the body and mind pure. Study the scriptures. Worship God; and do not utter useless words.'

These disciplines are the Yama and Niyama of Patanjali in a slightly expanded form. These are meant to purify the body and mind. Further steps follow: 'Adopt an easy, steady posture; slowly regulate the breath; withdraw the mind from senseobject'. These are the same as Asana, Pranayama and Pratyahara of the Yoga school. These are meant to turn the mind inwards.

The instruction continues: 'Fix the Prana and the mind on any of the centres of Prana such as Anahata or Visuddha. Meditate on Vishnu and His sports, and keep the mind constantly at peace. By these and other similar disciplines restrain the mind from its waywardness, regulate the breath and slowly, steadily and deliberately fix the mind on the blissful Lord.'

These are the last three steps of the Ashtangayoga, namely, Dharana, Dhyana and Samadhi which stand for different degrees of concentration. Whereas Patanjali recommends a flame, a pure heart or any other noble object for meditation, Kapila here prescribes a positive divine form to meditate upon. The purpose of meditation is gradual divinisation and ultimate elimination of the mind. The Bhagavata method serves that end better and that is the uniqueness of the Yoga of the Bhagavata.

Kapila gives a few more details about the various steps: 'Sitting on a comfortable seat in an easy posture, with the body neck and head held erect in a line. practise the control of breath. Breath in; retain the air inside and then expel the air and clear the air-passage; it may be done in the reverse order also. Restraint of breath purifies the mind just as fire fed by air removes the dross from metal ore. By the process of Pranayama etc., rid the body of its humoural imbalance. Burn the sins by Dharana; do away with sense-contact by Pratyahara — withdrawal of mind from external objects and turning it inward. Wipe off the stains of past impressions by Dhyana. With a calm and composed mind, meditate on the blissful form of the Lord.'

The various steps of the ladder of Yoga have been indicated. Now follows a pen-picture of an enchanting divine form the aspirant is advised to dwell upon.

Kapila continues: 'Meditate on the divine Lord having a smiling face charming as a lotus, with eyes red like the lotus, wearing the conch, disc, mace and lotus, in His four hands and with the hue of a blue lotus. Meditate on Him draped in yellow-silk with a Srivatsa mark adorning His chest and the Kaustubha jewel dangling from His neck. Meditate on Him wearing floral wreath of wild flowers with humming black bees, decked in a priceless necklace of pearls, bracelet, armlets, and tiara. Meditate on Him dazzling with the golden waist-band, seated in the hearts of devotees, supremely calm, a feast unto the eyes and the mind and with ravishing beauty. Meditate on Him of the most beautiful form, worshipped always by all, of tender age, and eager to bestow blessings of His devotees. Meditate on Him of holy fame worthy to be sung, Him who bestows glory on His votaries. Meditate on His full form like this till the mind is firmly fixed on Him.

After presenting a beautiful picture of the full form of Vishnu, Kapila goes on to describe each and every limb of the Lord for the devotee to fix his mind more intently upon. The melody and charm of those verses defy any attempt at translation. He concludes the instruction in the following words: 'Thus when the heart of the devotee melts through intense devotion to Hari, his body is clothed in horripilation owing to supreme happiness and he is bathed in tears of ectasy, then the hook of the mind also slowly drops off. When the mind becomes devoid of its hold, it gets dissolved like fire when the fuel is finished. The soul espies itself freed from the coverings of body, mind and other products of Prakriti. He then with the final disappearance of the mind attained after long and steady discipline and being established in the ultimate beatitude beyond pleasure and pain, comes to know that the real cause of pain and pleasure that had plagued him so long was the illusory ego. The self-illumined man will no more be aware whether the body which ferried him across Samsara remains or drops off, just as a drunken man is not aware whether he be draped or stripped. His body may remain alive as long as the Karmic impulses continue. But the illumined one does not identify himself with the body any more just as awakened man is not troubled by the dream objects. However much a man may be attached to his sons and wealth, he is distinctly separate from them, even so is an illumined soul from his erstwhile body. Just as all creatures are composed of the five elements, even so the same soul indwells all beings and all beings are seen superimposed in one and the same soul.' (Bh. 3.28. 1-42)

The goal of Yoga is the attainment of the one Supreme Soul. As paths, Yogas differ. The man of intellect, by analysis, denies ultimate being to the phenomena, and asserts his subjective, eternal being. The Yogi, through psychological processes stills the mind and projects the eternal Witness. The man of action prepares the ground for the progress of the soul. The Yoga expounded by Kapila in the Bhagavata is an integrated one; it incorporates the practical disciplines prescribed by Patanjali into the supreme love of God of Narada, thereby escaping the dryness that accompanies a purely psychological process and making the path smooth and sweet in the beginning, in the middle and in the end. Herein Kapila, Patanjali, Narada, Suka, and Vyasa meet, mingle and mix and they finally dissolve in the supreme syrup of *Sat-chid-ananda*. □

Dharana:
Some Yogic Practices

SWAMI SOMESWARANANDA

Dharana means retention of the mind. The beginners find it tremendously difficult to concentrate their mind or meditate. It is because they pass by without practising dharana. Dharana is the sixth stage of the eight-fold Yoga system prescribed by Patanjali. Unless one is adept in the sixth, one cannot jump into the seventh stage i.e. *dhyana*. So the beginners, in trying to meditate, actually practise *pratyahara* and *dharana*. They try to concentrate their mind but after sometime some foreign thoughts come. What do they do then? They try to take away their mind from the foreign thoughts and again try to retain their mind on the object of meditation. The first action is Pratyahara whereas the second is Dharana. In fact, Dharana is concentration and Dhyana is meditation.

Now, the Yogis have prescribed many techniques which are helpful to Dharana. Here in this essay we shall discuss some of those. Instead of practising Dharana subjectively it is better for the beginner to take the help of the sense-organs. Retain the mind on an external object with the help of sense-organs, then take the chakras (nervous plexus), and ultimately proceed to Dhyana.

Mind is easily attracted by the sense-object relation. We have got five Jnanendriyas, viz. eye, ear, nose, tongue, and skin. Through these senses we experience sight, sound, smell, taste, and touch respectively. Take up any sense-organ and keep it engaged with its specific perceptual object.

Through the eyes:

Take a picture, photo, or an idol of your *ishta* (chosen deity) and look at it. See His, Her feet, body, face — one by one, or all at a time. This is a simple process. But there is a particular yogic practice which is called *trataka* (to gaze steadily).

Trataka can be practised with black dot, candle flame, bright metal etc. Take a white paper and put a black dot of half-an-inch

diameter on it. Fix the paper in such a way that
the spot is some two feet away in front of your
eyes. If you practise Trataka sitting daily in a
particular place, you can make the black spot
on the white wall. Now fix your gaze on the
spot. Try not to wink and keep your look steady
and intent. If the eyes get watered or eye-lids
droop, take rest for a while and practise again.
After some days you will find it easy to keep
your eyes open even for 7-8 minutes. During
this practice you should not think of anything
else but the black spot. If the spot appears to be
doubled in size or number, if you see anything
else except the spot, please do not get dejected.
Close your eyes for a while and then again start
doing Trataka.

Instead of a black spot one can take the
help of a candle-flame also. Make the room
dark, light a candle, and look at the flame and
do Trataka.

One should practise Trataka both morning
and evening, for at least 15 minutes at a time.
It helps to retain the mind, but aspirants with
defective eye-sight should not practise it unless

under the guidance of a competent guide or guru.

Trataka can also be practised with a bright metal or a crystal, even on a black spot on the thumb. If one tries to look intently into these objects, one will acquire psychic powers. But here we do not like to discuss those practices as they may cause harm to the beginners. One should keep in mind that Trataka is a sort of Dharana which helps to make the mind steady. The steady mind helps one to meditate — the ultimate aim being *atma-jnana*.

Through the ear:

Try to concentrate on a continuous stream of sound as the buzz of a closed radio station or on the whispering sound of an electric fan. But it is best to concentrate on the *anahata-dhvani*. *Nadi-suddhi* helps one to hear the *anahata dhvani*.

As in *pranayama* there are three stages — *puraka*, *rechaka*, and *kumbhaka* — in *nadi-suddhi* there are only two viz. *puraka* and *rechaka*. Close the right nostril and inhale for 12 seconds through the left. Then close the left

nostril and exhale the air through the right for
12 seconds again. Now again inhale through the
right for the same duration and finally exhale
through the left for 12 seconds. These make
one round of *nadi-suddhi*. Please note that
there is no Kumbhaka in it. Start with five
rounds at a time and practise it in the morning,
at noon, in the evening, and at midnight. After
three months you will hear a particular sound in
the right ear. In fact this is not Anahata-dhvani
but a predecessor to it. One may concentrate on
this sound which goes on incessantly. At first
the sound seems like that of a cricket or a
humming bee. When concentration becomes
deep the sound seems like that of a bell or a
conch. To an advanced practitioner it appears
to shift its place from the right ear to the back
of the head, and then one feels that the sound
is coming out of the backbone. If one tries to
find out the source of this sound one feels it
coming from the heart or navel. To practise this
sort of Dharana one should keep one's eyes
closed and sit keeping the backbone straight.

Through the nose:

The technique of practising Dharana with

the help of the organ of smell is different from the two previous ones. Sitting on an *asana* and keeping the eyes closed, try to feel the incoming and outgoing breath. One is to concentrate on the breathing process though it has nothing to do with pranayama. One, initiated by a guru, should rather try to repeat his *mantra* during this practice. Instead of repeating the whole mantra at a time it is better to divide it. Say, one's mantra is 'Om Siva'. During the inhalation he should chant 'Om' once and during the exhalation 'Siva' once. Thus one inhalation and one exhalation make one round of breathing and one round of Japa. This is very helpful for the devotees. Practising this process for a month one can reverse the process of chanting mantra (i.e. Om during the exhalation and Siva during the inhalation). This is the primary step of the *Ajapa-japa* practice.

Through the tongue:

A spiritually advanced person sometimes feels in his mouth a sort of pleasing taste like that of honey or the sweet taste of fruits juice when he practises meditation. He may

concentrate on this taste also which is called
divya-svada (divine taste).

Those who do not experience this divine
taste may concentrate on the sensation of the
tongue touching the palate.

Through the skin:

Lie down on the bed. Relax. Become aware
of the meeting points between the body and the
bed. Concentrate on this awareness.

Or, keep an object near your seat. Touch
it and close the eyes. Become aware of your
touching the object. Concentrate on this
awareness.

Higher Practices:

Practice of Dharana through the
sense-organs, by one or more of the above-said
processes, is suitable for a beginner though
experience of the Anahata-Dhvani may be a bit
difficult for him. If one is adept in any of the
above-mentioned Dharanas, Dhyana will be
easier for him.

Let us now proceed to the advanced type
of Dharana. The practices discussed so far may
be termed as *sthula* (gross) *dharana*. Now let us

discuss the *sukshma-dharana* (subtle practices).

Close the eyes. Sit erect. Visualise the darkness in the forehead. Do it in a relaxed mood. After some time you will see a light just like a star appearing and immediately going away. Later white clouds moving slowly in that darkness will appear, or you may see blue or orange coloured objects, even a mixture of different colours, or sometimes light like the sun or the moon. Do not try to interpret or analyse these light or forms, nor look intently. Just watch like a witness. If no light is seen do not get dejected, visualise the darkness only.

If the aspirant finds it difficult to practise even Dharana, he should not give up. 'I cannot make my mind steady' — is a common complaint from a novice. Well, he should not get depressed at this but should try again. If the mind does not get steady, do not mind but observe the goings on in your mind. Watch carefully. You will see that some foreign thoughts are coming and disturbing you. Watch again. What do you see? One thought appears in your mind, rests for some time, and then it disappears. Another thought comes, resting for a while it also disappears. Watch the mind. You will find that a portion of the mind is being transformed into various thoughts, and another portion watches these thoughts. Is it not? You always experienced this, only were never conscious of it. Now if you look intently you will find that the portion which watches the thoughts, seems to be steady in comparison to the incoming and outgoing thought-waves. Try to concentrate on this steady portion of the mind. At first it may seem difficult, but gradual practice will not only make the mind steady but will lead the aspirant towards Dhyana also. This steady portion of the mind, which is in fact the I-awareness, should be caught hold of. This practice will lead the aspirant to the stage where he will feel himself as an awareness — only an awareness of I-ness will remain, the mind being devoid of thoughts. Then he will enter a higher stage of Dhyana where he will feel 'I am knowing or feeling myself'. Further he will feel only 'I am', and then only 'am'. At this stage if he visualizes a b-i-g black d-e-e-p hole appearing to engulf his whole existence he should try not to get frightened and face it

boldly. If he can face it, he will be absorbed in
samadhi.

Here two more Dharanas can be described:
tattva-dharana and *chidakasa-dharana*. Though
in Yoga-scriptures these are termed as
Dharana, yet these are in fact two Yogic
practices which lead the aspirant to the inner
depths of his mind and thus help him to know
some underlying truths.

Tattva-dharanas:

There are five Tattvas (elements; in fact
these are the five states) viz. *kshiti* (solid), *apa*
(liquid), *teja* (fiery), *marut* (gaseous), and
vyoma (space). According to Yoga these five
Tattvas can be realized in the first five *cakras*
(nervous plexus). If one concentrates on these
chakras, repeating the respective *bija-mantra*,
one after another, he will be able to get his mind
stronger to perceive subtle things. However,
here we do not like to discuss how subtle
psychic powers can be achieved by practising
Tattva Dharana. We shall mention only how to
practise the simple form of this *sadhana*.

Sit erect. Try to concentrate on the
muladhara (roughly, the lowest bone on the

backbone); imagine that there is the Kshiti-tattva — bright golden in colour and square in form — and mentally repeat its Bija-mantra 'Lam'. Do it for a minute, and then shift to the *svadhishthana* chakra (a little higher than the Muladhara and lower than the navel). Imagine the Apa-Tattva there — crescent formed, white coloured — and repeat the Bija 'Vam'. After a minute go up to the *manipura* chakra. It is just in the same line of the navel and posited in the backbone. Imagine the Teja-tattva there — bright red in colour, and looks like a triangle upside down — and repeat the Bija 'Ram' for the same duration. Next rise to the *anahata* chakra which is on the same line of the heart and posited in the backbone. Imagine Marut-tattva there — hexagonal in form and smoky-in colour — and repeat the Bija 'Yam' for 5 minutes. After that comes the *visuddhi* chakra — near the throat and in the backbone. Imagine the Vyoma-tattva there. This Tattva has no particular form but looks like the sky with various colours. Repeat the Bija 'Ham' for 5 minutes. Lastly rise to the *ajna* chakra. Its position is not like the above-said chakras. If you pierce the mid-point of your eye-brows with a stick and again pass another stick to pass through your left to come out of the right, the point where these two sticks will touch each other is roughly the position of the Ajna chakra. Imagine a small Siva-linga there — bright white in colour — and repeat the Pranava 'Om' for 5 minutes. Practise this sadhana either in the early morning or at mid-night.

The aspirant should note that it is better not to concentrate on either the Muladhara or Svadhishthana, even on the Manipura, for a long time as it may arouse baser passions in a novice. Anahata is the safest and best place. When practising Tattva-dharana beginners should not concentrate on the first three chakras for more than a minute each. Those who do their regular spiritual practice in the heart, they may increase the time for the Marut-tattva, and those who generally meditate on the Ajna Chakra, may increase the time to concentrate on the Siva-linga. During this practice the aspirant may visualize the forms of the Tattvas or bright forms of the sense-organs. It is a good sign. Analysing these forms one may know the condition of his mind and body. *Svarodaya Yoga* has dealt with it.

Chidakasa-dharana:

In discussing the Tattva-dharana we have mentioned six chakras, from Muladhara to Ajna. Here we like to note some more positions required for Chidakasa-dharana. *Sahasrara* is at the top of the head. *Bindu* is not a chakra. It is imagined just above the head. *Bhru-madhya* is the mid-point of the eye-brows. *Nasikagra* is the tip of the nose *Chidakasa* is in the forehead. If one closes one's eyes, one sees darkness. This darkness appears in the Chidakasa. The practitioner should note these eleven points or positions carefully — Muladhara, Svadhisthana, Manipura, Anahata, Visuddhi, Ajna, Sahasrara, Bindu, Chidakasa, Bhrumadhya and Nasikagra.

Now, to the practice. Sit erect and close your eyes. Follow the instructions one after another.

(1) Inhale air through the nose (using both the nostrils). Exhale slowly with the mantra 'Om'. During the exhalation imagine that the sound (Om) is coming up piercing the chakras

— from Muladhara to Svadhishthana, then to Manipura, Anahata, Visuddhi, Ajna and lastly to Sahasrara. Do this for thirteen times.

(2) Now concentrate on the Nasikagra then Bhrumadhya, Chidakasa, Sahasrara, Bindu, Ajna, Visuddhi, Anahata, Manipura, Svadhishthana, and Muladhara — one after another. Concentration on each point should not be for more than 15 seconds. Now concentrate in the opposite manner, that is first on the Muladhara, then Svadhishthana, Manipura etc-till the Nasikagra one after another again each for some 15 seconds. This up-and-down process makes one round. Practise three rounds.

(3) Now to the next step. Inhale vigorously and imagine that your breath is going from the Nasikagra to Bhrumadhya, then to Chidakasa, Sahasrara and ultimately to the Bindu. Stop breathing and concentrate on the Bindu for five seconds. During this concentration attract the navel backward (with the help of *uddiyana-bandha* and also attract the anus upward (with the help of *mulabandha mudra).* After five seconds exhale vigorously.

During this exhalation imagine that the breath is piercing through the Ajna, then Visuddhi, Anahata, Manipura, Svadhishthana, and finally Muladhara. Again stop breathing and concentrate on the Muladhara for a few seconds without any bandha or mudra. This whole process makes one round. Practise three rounds.

(4) Now concentrate according to the following directions one by one. Close your eyes. Try to forget that you have a body.

a) Visualise the darkness in the Chidakasa. If any colour or light appears just watch it as a witness. Look at the darkness and light as a mere witness. Do it for 5 minutes.

b) Imagine that your consciousness is moving forward penetrating the darkness. Go as far as you can. Do it for at least 10-15 minutes.

c) Look at the darkness in the Chidakasa — darkness in front, behind, above, below, dark all around. Try to take an over-all survey of the darkness.Now imagine yourself as a speck of light and that there is infinite darkness all around you. Think that there is nothing, no world, no stars, n-o-t-h-i-n-g; only darkness and you at its centre as a point of light. Do it for 10-15 minutes.

   d) Imagine your *ista-devata* (chosen deity) in the Chidakasa.

   (5) Repeat the process No.1 with inhalation-exhalation and chanting *Om* as described earlier.

   (6) Pray to the ishta-devata.

   (7) Make the mind empty.

   (8) Do Japa for 5 minutes.

This is a higher type of Yogic practice which makes the mind subtle and expands the consciousness.

Conclusion

Here in this article we have discussed many Yogic practices for Dharana. An aspirant need not practise all these. He may choose any one of these that suits him most. We should keep in mind that our intention is to make the mind fit for Dhyana and therefore we have described these techniques in their simplest forms. These are all separate practices, and if one practises these, all or any one of these, one will be able to explore the psychic layers and powers and know the role of mind, one's personality, and at the same time one can discover the underlying truths or the mystery of the mind. Trataka and Nadi-shuddhi have therapeutic value also. Tattva-dharana and Chidakasa-dharana are higher Yogic practices and so it is better to practise these under the guidance of a competent teacher. To do these practices the aspirant will face some obstacles or difficulties according to his past impressions *(samskaras)*. It is better for a practitioner to discover these obstacles himself. He will realize the underlying truths himself. These obstacles and illuminations are not described here, not even the theoretical side of these practices for paucity of space. It needs a separate article to discuss all these. There are some more Yogic practices like these which are of higher order and certainly need a Guru to guide. It is not wise to practise these higher.Yogic sadhanas without a competent teacher as these involve many intricacies and if not done properly these may affect the aspirant's health adversely. Yoga is a psycho-physical process and so it has effect on both the body and the mind. So it is better to practise Yoga under a guide. ☐

Yoga: Neurophysiological Basis

DR. B. RAMAMURTHI

Introduction:

Four millennia ago India has given to the world the supreme science viz. Yoga Sastra, also known as Atma Vidya. The ancient thinkers of our great land sought and found something beyond the everyday existence which most mortals seem destined to live on this earth viz, birth, growth, procreation and death, caught in the coils of emotional tangles, apparently meaningless and all ephemeral. The Rishis became aware of great possibilities of mental and physical achievements far beyond the apparent level of our existence. At these high levels, Joy becomes supreme, Existence itself becomes a Joy and an everlasting Truth. They demonstrated by personal example that such levels of achievements are within reach of ordinary human beings. They also handed down to numerous succeeding generations the principles, the practices and the techniques of Yoga through Yoga Sutras.

Psychobiological Basis

As time rolled on, the practioners of Yoga began to envisage a psychobiological complex in the human body, depending on the various levels of concentration of energy fields and described as chakras. The most commonly prevailing concept was that a great energy field was lying latent in the lower part of the human body (the Kundalini) awaiting to be released, awaiting to be converted from a potential and latent form into an active and energetic form capable of reactivating and restructuring all the systems in the body including the higher levels of thinking namely Manas and Buddhi and Ahankara. Trainees and aspirants were encouraged to feel such energisation in their own system.

Each level of energy field or chakra was elaborately described and allotted to a particular situation in the human body. In addition in Yogic psychophysiology, there are two vertically running energy fields, the *ida* and *pingala* which play a vital role in health, disease and in supramental achievements. Except for a broad resemblance to multifaceted brain on top (i.e. Sahasrara chakra) and the spinal cord lower down, there was no actual physical correlation in the Rishis' minds with the organic nervous system existing in the body. In fact, while knowledge and experience of psychic levels of energy fields seems to have been fully realised and appreciated. There was apparently no detailed knowledge about the brain or the nervous system among the ancients. We see only a few references to the brain, spinal cord and nerves in our literature on Yoga and Ayurveda. Apparently our Rishis and Yogis concentrated on the psychological energy fields rather than the organic anatomy and physiology of our nervous system.

The Human Brain—A Highly Complex System

Our present-day knowledge of this fascinating organ, the Human Brain, is only about 230 years old. During these two centuries we have acquired a very large amount of knowledge about the function and structure of this most marvellous piece of equipment. With physics, chemistry, mathematics and technology advancing by leaps and bounds the understanding of brainfunction has also advanced, though we are still far from unravelling all its mysteries.

The human brain consists of more that 1000 million cells which are termed neurons in addition to having a similar number of supporting cells called glial cells. Each neuron has a long tension process the axon along which it sends messages and a number of small projections called dendrons through which each neuron receives messages from other cells. There could be anything between 10 to 50 such connections between different cells. One can imagine the number of permutations and combinations that are possible for energy transfer through a system consisting of 1000 million units or more and where each unit can make anything between 10 to 50 connections. The possibilities are really astronomical.

Electrochemical Basis:

As far as our present knowledge goes energy generation in the brain is through an electrochemical complex. Shifting of the sodium and potassium ions from the inside and outside of the cells creates an electrical potential which travels down the axons and initiates action in another neuron or in an organ like muscle or gland. The connecting region between the nerve ending and other nerve cells or organs is known as the synapse. These synapses are controlled by chemical regulators known as neurotransmitters. By altering the chemistry in and around the synapses, the transfer of messages from one cell to another can be greatly modified. The variety and preferential site of action of many neurotransmitters are gradually being clarified thus enlarging our concept of brain function at the higher levels.

By a series of intervening processes which are not very clear, this whole electrochemeical complex of neurons of the brain is capable of not only regulating ordinary functions like breathing, moving about, eating etc., but also is responsible for memory, emotions and higher intelligence.

Localisation

From various experiments as well as from human observations we are now aware which parts of the brain are responsible for different functions like hearing, vision, memory, intelligence, judgement, emotion etc. The left brain is important for speech whereas the right brain is important for understanding nonverbal images and ideas. Of course the two halves work in close liaison through a big bundle of associating fibre connections bridging the two halves of the brain. The frontal lobes serve intelligence and judgement, the temporal lobes serve memory and the rear portion of the brain is necessary for vision. Though each area of the brain has a specific function it must be emphasised that most often the brain functions as a single unit due to the intricate interconnection between all the areas.

The Upper and the Lower Brain

Compared to the lower animals, it is in the human that the cerebral cortex (the upper and outermost part of the brain) has expanded enormously and contains many times more neurons and synapses than the nearest apes. In spite of such expansion of the cerebral cortex, the main source of energy and drive lies in the emotional system of the brain and in one small area in the centre of the brain known as the hypothalamus. These areas are responsible for emotions like love, hatred, fear, anger, etc. They also control hunger, thirst, sex drive and procreational processes in the body.

Still the lower brain rules and aggression prevails.

In spite of many thousands of years of evolution and in spite of the marked development of the upper brain, the behavioural pattern of the majority of human beings is under the control of the lower emotional brain and the hypothalamus. This leads to the distressing phenomenon of the severe aggressiveness exhibited by the human races, the only creation on earth that kills its own kind. In the whole animal kingdom it is very rare to see an animal killing its own kind for gain or in any fight. This does not refer of course to the natural instinct of animals to kill certain other kinds of animal for food. Usually when a fight ensues between animals of the same kind, the defeated animal runs away. It is not pursued and killed by the victor. Why is it that man alone does this? At the same time we learn from history as well as from experience that some human beings are also capable of supreme love and sacrifice. Here lies an enigma that so far our modern scientific knowledge of brain functions or of psychology has not been able to solve.

Evolutionally speaking, as the outer brain i.e. the cerebral cortex which is responsible for the intelligence, judgement, reason etc. expanded, its powers should have grown to such an extent that it could easily control the emotional level of existence. But in practice this has not been so. Perhaps this may be due to the nondevelopment of the controlling power of the upper brain over the lower brain. In other words, though the structure and the organisation for the higher control of emotions exists in the brain, in practice it has not functioned.

Yoga corrects the imbalance

It is in this context that we are able to view today the practical usefulness of Yoga as an everyday science and as an everyman's science. Yoga is not something esoteric or highbrow which is within the reach of only a chosen few. It is apparent that the practice of Yoga leads to an establishment of the superiority of the upper brain over the lower brain and thus releases one from the shackles of everyday fear, anger, hatred and attachment.

There can be no doubt that Yoga improves the functioning of the brain. This has been observed in the EEG patterns of Yogis where one can see the greater correlation and synchronization of the electrical activity of the brain. Acting through the nervous system, Yoga also favourably affects the functioning of all the other systems in the body. This has again been proved conclusively by experimental observations. Studies have shown that the biogenic amines and the neurotransmitters in the nervous system get altered during deep meditation. During Yogic · practices, the functional hierarchy of the nervous system gets reoriented, and functions, hitherto known as autonomic, come under the control of the Cortex or (Will). Taking the practice of Pranayama as an example, complete control is super-imposed by the Yogi over breathing. Normally breathing is mostly involuntary, though voluntary control can be imposed for a short time. The process of respiration is under control of the medulla oblongata, autonomic nerves and also the chemicals circulating in the body. By Pranayama exercises this function is gradually freed from the lower controls and brought under the Will of the Yogi.

Awakening the dormant power:

The structure and the function of the brain as understood by us today leads one to believe that the ordinary human being uses only a small part of the potential power lying dormant in this masterpiece of creation. If one could use some more of this potential power our existence on this earth will become more meaningful and joyful. It is our firm belief that Yoga does exactly this, namely to make us utilise the power that we already have.

Hope for the Future:

Viewing the proneness of human beings to hurt and destroy their environment and their own kind by monstrous weapons, one feels that hope for the future of the human race lies only in improving our brain power in the proper direction. This can only be achieved by following the various tenets of Yoga which have been propounded in detail by our great seers; therein lies salvation for the human race. ☐

Attainment of Yoga

Maladies and Remedies

SWAMI HARSHANANDA

A millionaire once asked his son to prepare
a list of all the things he would like to possess
in order to be happy. Very enthusiastically the
boy prepared and brought a long list of
seventeen items. After scanning it, the father
scored it all off with his red pencil and wrote the
words "PEACE OF MIND" in big letters. Then
he advised him thus: "My dear boy! Even after
possessing all these seventeen things, if you
have no peace of mind they are worthless. If,
on the other hand, you have peace of mind,
these seventeen will become irrelevant!" What
a wonderful insight into life!

Knowingly or unknowingly, all of us are
struggling to get peace. As long as our mind is
in pieces and the pieces are in ceaseless mutual
conflict, peace eludes us. It is only when we
learn to put these pieces together so as to make
the mind whole and integrated that we gain the
peace of Kaivalya.

This is easier said than done. However, with competent guides like Patanjali who are ever eager to help out of infinite compassion, this task should not be that difficult.

Patanjali, the great master of the Yoga system, calls these pieces of the mind as vrttis, modifications, which are ever arising and never subsiding. Yoga or union (yuj = to yoke) of the individual self with the Supreme Self will result through Yoga or Samadhi, (yuj = to get samadhi or perfect concentration) when these Vrttis are controlled, supressed and eliminated, by the right kind of discipline and training. This discipline and training is also Yoga.

One who wants to be healthy and strong should be well aware of the diseases and debilities which destroy health. After all, prevention is better than cure! Similarly one who wants Yoga should be fully aware of the factors that destroy Yoga, or, those that are not conducive to it. Patanjali, with his highly scientific outlook, has systematically listed these factors which he has termed as Antarayas ('intruders in the path of Yoga'). He has divided these into two groups. He calls the first as

'Antarayas' and the second as 'Vikshepasahabhuvah' (co-existing with mental distraction).

The 'Antarayas' are nine *(vide* Yoga Sutras 1.30): Vyadhi (disease), Styana (mental laziness), Samsaya (doubt), Pramada (heedlessness), Alasya (physical laziness), Avirati (absence of dispassion), Bhrantidarsana (false perception), Alabdha-bhumikatva (non-attainment of Yogic states) and Anavasthitatva (falling away from Yogic states when obtained). Let us now consider them one by one.

1. **Vyadhi** (physical disease): Ayurveda, the Hindu science of health and longevity, defines physical disease as the condition of imbalance of the three basic humours of the body viz., Vata (the wind), Pitta (the bile) and Sleshma (the phlegm). Uneven flow and distribution of the Rasa (chemicals produced by food and drink) as also the shortage or surfeit of the sense organs is another cause of disease. Since the body and mind are closely interconnected, it is but natural that diseases of the body disturb the mind making it almost

impossible to practise Yoga. Hence curing the disease, restoring, rebuilding health and strength is a must for Yoga. Apart from medicines, diet and following the rules of health and sanitation, the practice of asanas, can be of great help in this direction. The asanas, often being imitations of the posture of birds and animals, can give not only health and vigour but also the particular ability of body for which the particular animal (whose posture is being imitated) is well known. The advice of Lord Sri Krishna to the Yogi to be moderate in eating, sleeping, recreation and work, since excesses destroy health, making it impossible to practise Yoga (vide Gita 6.16,17), is very relevant in this context.

2. **Styana** (mental laziness): The mind is an expert in playing tricks. Also it is very choosy. It jumps to activity when there are prospects of pleasure or immediate results. Where and when sustained hard work is needed, just it stays put! It is human nature to desire good results without taking the trouble to do good, and to abhor evil results without taking

the trouble to avoid evil. (On the other hand people often go out of the way to commit sins!).

The only way of conquering the evil is by cultivating discrimination and will power. Discrimination gives the conviction that Yogic disciplines help in achieving concentration and peace. Once the conviction arises, the mind must be forced to do the bidding of its master, the Sadhaka (spiritual aspirant).

Development of will power is a problem that is often faced by everyone of us. If we can exercise our body and build up its strength gradually, there is no reason why the same cannot be done with our mind! By denying ourselves small pleasures and temptations to begin with, we can gradually but surely build up our will power. The example given by the Holy Mother of the farmer who could lift a bull because he used to carry it daily since the time it was a small helpless calf, can give us much-needed encouragement here also.

3. **Samsaya** (doubt): In any new field of venture doubts and misgivings are always there. When it concerns a field like that of control and

concentration of mind which is purely intangible and subtle, the rising of doubts is inevitable. The field of operation of such doubts is almost unlimited. Starting with doubting the veracity of the scriptures and the Guru and extending it to one's capacity for achieving Yoga, it can end in doubting one's own very existence! While observing that the ignorant, the unbelieving and the doubting people, will ruin themselves, Lord Sri Krishna comes down heavily on the last group by asserting that they lose both this world and the next **(Gita 4.40).**

Cultivation of Sraddha or faith in the holy books, the spiritual teacher and oneself, is the only antidote for this malady. One should impress upon oneself that even day-to-day life is not possible without faith in one's relatives, friends and neighbours. How much more faith, then, is needed in spiritual life, which is a journey into the unseen and unknown?

4. Pramada (heedlessness): If eternal vigilance is the price of freedom, it is even more so the price one should pay to get spiritual freedom. Here absence of vigilance will inevitably lead to Samsara (the eternal rounds of births and deaths). That is why the great sage Sanatsujata goes to the extent of declaring that Pramada is itself Mrtyu death) (*vide* Sanatsujatiya 1.4).

Pramada constitutes forgetfulness and heedlessness with regard to the knowledge and cultivation of virtues like Ahimsa (non-injury) and Satya (truth) which are declared as the means to Yoga. Unless they are assiduously cultivated and protected, Yoga is not possible. Any lack of vigil will lead to quick and steep fall in spiritual life like the fall of the ball that slips out of the hands of a careless child playing with it at the top of a staircase (*vide.* Vivekachudamani 324). Much care is bestowed in the world on petty pelf and filthy lucre. Should not at least an equal amount of care be bestowed on the means of Yoga which is spiritual wealth?

5. Alasya (physical laziness): There is a witty saying that laziness travels so slowly that poverty soon overtakes it! If laziness is thus the enemy of even Preyas (worldly well-being) how much more is it so with regard to Sreyas (things spiritual)? The only way to overcome laziness is by engaging oneself in healthy activities including service to others.

6. **Avirati** (absence of dispassion): Yoga concerns things spiritual. Yoga is perfect concentration on the self leading to self-realisation. This is impossible unless the mind is drained of all its dross. Attachment to the non-self, things mundane, lust and lucre as Sri Ramakrishna puts it, is the dross. God and mammon cannot go together. So the aspirant after Yoga must relentlessly practise detachment and dispassion. As in the case of the development of will power, here also detachment can be built up starting the practice with smaller things. But this is only the negative side. The positive side, seeing real danger in objects of temptation through cultivation of discrimination, is the better way.

7. **Bhrantidarsana** (false perception): This and the next two obstacles are more serious, hence needing greator effect and more tactful handling. At the intellectual

level, false perception can manifest itself as misunderstanding the teachings of the guru and the scripture. This can be due to dullness or perversion of intellect. More often it is due to self-conceit. In any case question and discussions with the Guru in all humility will solve this problem.

False perception is possible at the psychic level also. Wrong methods of practice can lead to hallucinations, which can be remedied only by consulting the Guru or souls advanced in spiritual life. But then, how to know whether a psychic experience is true or false? True experience gives joy and peace whereas the false one may not have any impact or may even cause unhappiness, fears and tensions.

Psychic experiences like clairvoyance and clairaudience, though true in themselves, can produce a false sense of self-realisation thus blocking further progress. This is akin to the foolishness of the man who missed the train by whiling away his time on the roadside magic show! It needs great strength and wisdom to transcend the temptations of such psychic powers as often develop as a matter of course

in spiritual aspirants. Patanjali himself warns
the aspirants against this danger in Su.3.51
'When supernatural beings occupying celestial
spheres invite the Yogi (to their worlds) he
should neither be tempted nor puffed up with
pride, since there is every possibility of a fall
into Samsara.'

8. Alabdhabhumikatva (non-attainment
of Yogic states): In spite of the fact that the
aspirant is correctly practising the various steps
and disciplines of Yoga, he fails to attain any of
the Yogabhumis (planes of psychic and
spiritual experiences) mentioned in the
textbooks of Yoga. The malady behind this
frustration and its remedy can be more easily
understood in the light of a fine parable of Sri
Ramakrishna. A farmer used to toil the whole
day and water his field. The next morning he
would find the field completely dry. Failing to
discover the reason, he sought the assistance of
his friend who showed him some rat-holes
behind a bush, which were swallowing up all the
water. Once these rat-holes were sealed the
problem was solved. Similarly, there are
'rat-holes' in our personality which need

closing and sealing. Any deep-rooted evil tendency like inordinate attachment to lust and lucre or mercurial irritability or crass selfishness can be the 'rat-hole'. These evils often camouflage themselves as desirable virtues and so the aspirant fails to recognise them in their true colours. By dispassionate and deep introspection, consultation with the Guru and brother disciples, one can discover one's weaknesses and try to eliminate them, thereby quickening the progress.

9. **Anavasthitatva** (falling away from Yogic states when obtained): This obstacle is even more serious. With great difficulty the Yogi succeeds in raising his mind to certain higher states but very soon it slides back to lower ones or goes back into the old rut. It is like the mongoose to whose tail a piece of brick is tied by the mischievous children of the house. After great exertion when it reaches its hole near the roof of the hut, the weight of the brick piece pulls it back.

The reasons for one's fall are similar to the aforementioned while describing the previous obstacle. The 'brick' of old Samskaras (tendencies) has to be removed first.

To these nine obstacles, Patanjali adds five more classifying them separately as the second group. They are: Duhkha (sorrow), Daurmanasya (despondency), Angamejayatva (restlessness of limbs), Svasa (forcible inhalation) and Prasvasa (forcible exhalation). He calls these 'viksepasahabhuvah' (co-existing with mental distraction), because if they exist, they are immediately and invariably followed by mental distraction.

Duhkha (sorrow and suffering) can be caused by physical diseases and injuries, mental tensions, natural calamities and so on. As long as it exists the mind will be in a disturbed state making it impossible to pursue Yogic practices. Removal of the causes that give rise to Duhkha or enduring it patiently when found to be inevitable is the only remedy.

Daurmanasya   (disappointment) is caused by unfulfilled desires and ambitions. This will automatically lead to agitation in the mind. It is neither possible nor desirable to fulfil all our desires and ambitions. Hence one should take recourse to discrimination and be convinced that desire is the root cause of all our troubles. Once the intensity of desire is lessened, the shock of disappointment also will be lessened. If and when it is completely eliminated, the problem is permanently solved.

Angamejayatva . (restlessness of the limbs): When sorrow, disappointment and despair are not sublimated by discrimination and will power, they cause tremendous restlessness in the mind. This affects the nervous system getting reflected in physical restlessness. The aspirant is thus unable to sit steadily on the seat and frequently changes his position. Persisting in the practice of Yoga, of repetition of pranava (Om) and attitude of surrender to God will gradually lessen this disturbance.

Svasa and Prasvasa (forcible inhalation and exhalation): These are actually obstacles to the practice of pranayama. When the yogi wants to retain the breath, it is forcibly thrown out and when he wants to exhale the breath it is forcibly drawn in. This defect is due partly to mental restlessness and partly to lack of practice in pranayama. Apart from the methods mentioned previously for controlling the mind and reducing its restlessness, vigorous and regular practice of pranayama will restore the balance in breathing. This will again exert a sobering and calming effect on the mind.

So far, the fourteen obstacles listed by Patanjali, have been dealt with. Appropriate antidotes have also been suggested. But does Patanjali himself suggest directly or indirectly any method by which all these obstacles to yoga can be nullified and eliminated? We have some sutras which help us to solve this riddle.

Patanjali was obviously a devotee of God. This is why his Yoga system is known as 'Sesvara-Sankhya' (the Sankhya philosophy that accepts Iswara or God) as opposed to the Sankhya system which by contrast is labelled as Nirisvara-sankhya (the Sankhya that does not accept God). Patanjali, after dealing with the topic of Samadhi (perfect concentration giving super-conscious experiences) in great detail (1. 12 to 22), declares in the very next sutra that Samadhi can be obtained, alternatively, by devotion and surrender to God. If devotion to God can give even Samadhi, can it not give the much smaller result of the removal of obstacles to Yoga? Obviously it does. This he accepts in su.29, wherein he declares that meditation and devotion to God will remove all the obstacles to Yoga and give self-knowledge.

Obstacles and impediments are inevitable in every field of life and more so in the life of the spirit. As Swamiji puts it, "Great things can be done by great sacrifices only!" Hence the immensity or intensity of the obstacles should bestir the yogic aspirants to even greater efforts and more dogged persistence instead of dampening their spirits.   □

devotion and surrender to God. If devotion to God can give even Samadhi, can it not give the much smaller result of the removal of obstacles to Yoga? Obviously it does. Thus he accepts in sū.29, wherein he declares that meditation and devotion to God will remove all the obstacles to Yoga and give self-knowledge.

Obstacles and impediments are inevitable in every field of life and more so in the life of the spirit. As Swami Ram has it, "Great things can be done by great qualities only." Hence the immensity or intensity of the obstacles should turn the yogic aspirants to even greater efforts and more dogged persistence instead of dampening their spirits.   □